BASIC PRINCIPLES OF GEOCOSMIC STUDIES

FOR

FINANCIAL MARKET TIMING

BASIC PRINCIPLES OF GEOCOSMIC STUDIES

FOR

FINANCIAL MARKET TIMING

BY
RAYMOND A. MERRIMAN

SEEK-IT PUBLICATIONS P.O. BOX 250012 W. BLOOMFIELD, MI 48325

DISCLAIMER

All information provided herein is based upon original research and observations of Raymond A. Merriman. It is written with sincere and reliable intent.

Although these methods and techniques have proven reliable over the years, there cannot be and therefore is no guarantee that these same methods will continue to work in the future. Therefore neither the publisher nor the author assume any responsibility whatsoever for any reader's activity or decisions regarding trading or investing.

1st printing: June 1995
2nd printing: June 1999
3rd printing: September 2002
4th printing: May 2006

BASIC PRINCIPLES OF GEOCOSMIC STUDIES FOR FINANCIAL MARKET TIMING

Published in the United States by: MMA/Seek-It Publications
P.O. Box 250012
West Bloomfield, MI 48325
1-248-626-3034
Fax: 1-248-626-5674
Website: www.mmacycles.com

TABLE OF CONTENTS

Chapter One: Introduction To Geocosmic Studies and Financial Market Timing	1
Chapter Two: Getting Started: Using The Proper Tools	6
Chapter Three: Using The Ephemeris: Part I	9
Chapter Four: Understanding Planets	13
Chapter Five: The Signs of the Zodiac	24
Chapter Six: Using The Epehmeris Part II: Determining Aspects	29
Chapter Seven: Using The Aspectarian	35
Chapter Eight: Using Computers To Determine "Clusters"	43
Appendix: The Sign of the Zodiac in Astrology	48
References:	54

CHAPTER ONE

INTRODUCTION TO GEOCOSMIC STUDIES AND FINANCIAL MARKET TIMING

What you are about to read may totally change the way you think about financial market analysis.

The role of geocosmic studies in the field of market timing is not part of mainstream thought. Amongst the financial market community, the correlation tends to be even more arcane. Most market analysts have not pursued geocosmic studies at all, and they tend to believe that geocosmic signatures - as a market timing tool - may be akin to superstition, and practiced by individuals who are, at best, suffering from some sort of delusion. Even with those traders who are astrologically-oriented, there tends to be the opposite problem. They usually believe that geocosmic studies are a "stand alone" timing system for market analysis. Nothing could be further from the truth in both instances.

Those two extreme positions are jointly held by practitioners who have no personal experience in the other's field of expertise. So let us begin by explaining the *relationship of market timing to market analysis*, and then the *relationship of geocosmic signatures to market timing* as used by MMA, Inc., one of the leaders in "Market Timing" products and services throughout the world.

MMA's trading philosophy states that successful trading of financial and commodity markets depends upon three factors: (1) **accurate analysis**, (2) **a trading plan** that combines the signals generated by the analysis with proper risk management parameters, and (3) the **discipline** to follow the trading plan.

The first of these - *accurate analysis* - is the primary focus of MMA. You simply cannot be wrong consistently in the market and expect to be profitable.

Accurate market analysis itself depends upon three factors: **(1) Trend Analysis, (2) Market Timing, and (3) Technical Analysis.**

1. Trend Analysis: This is the art of determining the direction (bull or bear) of the market. Knowing whether an underlying trend is up (bull) or down (bear) is essential to proper analysis and trading success. Many different studies have many different criteria for identifying the underlying trend of a market. Some of these studies include: fundamental analysis, Elliot Wave analysis, Technical Analysis, and Cycles, to name just four.

2. Market Timing: Knowing when a market is likely to make a significant crest or trough is essential to proper market analysis and trading success. It is also very difficult. Again, there are many different studies that focus on market timing, and each has a different set of rules. Some of these studies include: Gann, Cycles, and Geocosmics. The latter involves the planetary studies of astrology.

3. Technical Analysis: Market reversals are oftentimes preceded by a change in momentum and/or inter-related market divergences. The study of these mathematically-calculated relationships in price or patterns can help one determine whether or not a price movement is significant.

All three of these forms of market analysis can be integrated. They can be supportive and complementary to one another. When they are, a powerful trading plan can be developed, one that will enhance a trader's probability of making successful decisions in the market place.

Now the question is: "What about astrology? What is the proper place of certain geocosmic signatures in the field of market analysis and successful trading?"

As you can see from the above description, geocosmic studies (and hence astrology) fall into the category of *market timing*. In that category, it is not alone. Gann and Cycles studies are also included in this department of *market timing* tools.

Of them all, geocosmic signatures are perhaps the most precise of the *market timing* tools. But keep in mind that these belong in the field of *market timing*. They do not effectively determine *trend* (as do studies in Trend Analysis), nor do they consistently determine *price* (as do studies in Technical Analysis). Geocosmic studies, in their purest and most usable application, are a study of *timing* changes in short-term trends, or "market reversals."

Besides being the most precise of all market timing tools, geocosmic studies have two other unique features that cause it to stand out: it is the least accepted (and hence least used), and it is perhaps the most difficult to learn of all studies in market analysis.

Geocosmic studies involve the use of astrological formulas and principles. More specifically they actually involve the use of astronomic bodies and principles, but since the study of astronomy applied to the human experience (and markets are a "human experience") comprises the definition of astrology, it is said to fall in the category of astrology. Mention the word "astrology" to someone who has never studied the subject, and chances are he/she does not consider it a serious study. In fact, for the past three centuries astrology has been incorrectly considered more a form of entertainment than a subject worthy of academic research efforts.

It wasn't always that way. In fact, astrology is the mother of astronomy, and the earliest astronomers were indeed astrologers. But astrology fell out of favor during the "Age of Reason". Science and Religion both agreed there was no place in society for a study that threatened the truths that these two other fields preached. Astrology came to be considered a "pseudo-science", and after generations of this stigma, it has remained out of academia - unchallenged, and un-investigated by the brilliant minds of successive generations for three centuries.

This omission of astrology as a legitimate study in society has some positives. Most notably, it represents a body of knowledge - and hence truth - that is virtually unexplored by today's populations, in a manner that may be applicable to today's world. In terms of financial and commodity markets, this means there is a vast area of study that can and does yield a whole host of valuable correlations to market timing that very few people know about. In fact, very few people care about the *possibility* of such a correlation, because it goes against either their beliefs, or "what they know to be true." It doesn't matter that they haven't studied the subject. The line separating truth and belief in today's world is sometimes very hard to define, much as is the difference between subjective and objective reality.

The second thing to know about Geocosmic analysis - especially as it pertains to financial and commodity markets - is that it is not an easy subject to learn. It means you have to learn the basic principles of astrology. Astrology is much more difficult to learn than any of the other subjects mentioned so far - Fundamental Analysis, Gann, Cycles, Trend Analysis, Technical Analysis, etc. This too keeps people from accepting it. Oftentimes they will begin to study it, thinking the subject of astrology must be easy to learn since it is not held in high regard by today's society. But along the way they realize it is not a simple subject. In fact, it is akin to learning a foreign language (the language of astronomic symbols, applied to the field of human affairs). It takes time. It takes concentration. It takes a certain amount of memorizing. It requires applying many, many combinations to yield a probable interpretation or possible result. It takes serious thinking and mental organization of various factors. For many who enter into the study, the tour is short-lived because it is difficult.

It is our hope that this book will make that journey a more simple and rewarding one than you would have otherwise embarked upon. We will attempt to make a difficult subject more simple and relevant to your needs as a trader seeking use of a very powerful market timing tool. In this regard, you do not have to know everything about astrology. There are certain areas, and certain beginning principles in Financial Astrology, that will be sufficient to increase your market timing skills. This book will cover the basic beginning principles necessary to get started. The content of this material then, will include the following topics:

- Tools To Get Started
- How To Read An Ephemeris
- Identifying and Understanding Planets
- Identifying the Signs of The Zodiac
- Using The Signs of the Zodiac As a Reference For Measuring Distances Between Planets
- Determining Aspects Between Planets
- Determining Ingresses
- Using an "Aspectarian"
- Determining "Clusters" and "Reversal Dates"
- Using Financial/Astrological Software Programs

Understanding aspects and ingresses are the keys to utilizing geocosmics principles in the field of "Market Timing." These principles can be taught in about 4-5 hours. However, to learn them properly, you will have to spend some time on these principles, going over and over the symbols and their meanings so that they become part of your automatic thinking process. You will have to eventually commit to memory the symbols and order of the planets and signs of the zodiac, which is much easier than it may sound at this moment. You will want to get past the point of having to look up a particular symbol in a book to find out what it means. Although this may sound hard, it is not. And one of the reasons why it is not hard is because this is truly a fascinating study. If it was boring, or irrelevant to your life, it would be hard and uninteresting. But that is not the case here. The study of geocosmic principles, and astrology, is ultimately a study about oneself, about one's world. Very few things are more exciting than experiencing a subject that yields personal revelation. And with an open mind, this study does just that.

CHAPTER TWO

GETTING STARTED: USE THE PROPER TOOLS

Getting started in the study of astrology applied to financial markets requires the use of proper tools. Nothing can be more frustrating than spending large sums of money and/or great amounts of time in learning something, only to later discover that you are working with inadequate tools. The best tools today, of course, are in computers and software programs. And of course the purchase of these tools can represent a considerable outlay of monies. Rather than starting out with a new computer and/or new and expensive software programs, we will recommend beginning just with the best basic essentials. After seeing whether or not this is indeed a field you wish to enter, you can then determine which - if any - software programs to purchase that will make your calculations and analysis tasks much simpler.

We will cover all ranges of tools available and necessary to utilize principles of geocosmic studies in market analysis that are presented in this book. You should also know that most of the tools and software programs recommended herein are available directly through MMA. Since most these tools are not readily available through traditional outlets, this may at times seem somewhat like a commercial. We apologize if that seems the case, but there is little value in describing an important tool you will need for this study if you cannot find that tool.

The simplest and most inexpensive way to get started is with the use of an ephemeris and a simple hand calculator. We will start here, knowing full well that many of you reading this book will eventually by-pass this section and purchase a good astrological software program. But even before you do that, understand that there is great value in learning and understanding the basic calculations that go into determining "aspects" - the most important key to geocosmic signatures related to market timing. By going over these processes, you will develop a comprehensive understanding and a greater skill at using this unconventional study in your analysis of financial markets.

A simple hand calculator is easy to purchase at any department, drug, or electronics store. Enough said. Just have it ready as we begin this learning experience.

An ephemeris is not so readily available. Let's first of all describe what an ephemeris is, and then where to get one, and finally, which one to get. An ephemeris is a book that contains the daily position of the planets, Sun, and Moon as seen from Earth. Usually these ephemerides are available in one-year increments, 10-year, or even one-century increments. Typically each page of an ephemeris contains one month of daily planetary positions (see example 1, page 10).

The ephemeris and calculator are all you need to begin the study of geocosmic signatures as they relate to financial markets. There are other books that may be very helpful in the understanding of basic astrological principles, which in turn could be useful in understanding concepts of financial astrology. These recommended texts include:

1. The Gold Book: Geocosmic Correlations to Gold Price Cycles by Raymond A. Merriman. It is a "classic that still works", has proved the test of time. The same geocosmic and cyclical principles laid down in that work in 1982, still work consistently today.

2. Basic AstroTech, by Jeanne Long. This primer shows the relationship of Gann studies to astrology for enhanced market timing.

3. The Only Way To Learn Astrology, Part I and II (and possibly the others), by Marion March and Joan McEvers. These books are especially useful to those who want to pursue astrological studies.

4. Merriman On Market Cycles: The Basics, by Merriman. This book covers the basic principles of Cycle Studies, another discipline in the field of market timing (it has nothing to do with astrology).

5. Secrets of a Silver Trader: The Sun, Moon, and Silver Market by Merriman. This book describes the relationship of the 2-1/2 day transits of the Moon through various signs of the zodiac, and is most useful to those who wish to utilize short-term timing techniques to trading Silver.

6. Any Year's ***Forecasts Book***, by Merriman. Available annually December 15: Specify year of choice, or next year's. This books covers a geocosmic interpretation of economic and market trends in effect for each given year.

7. ***The Universal Clock***, by Jeanne Long. This text shows the correlation between planetary degrees and prices of various stock indices and commodities.

If you find this book to be of interest and wish to continue with studies in this area, these are some of the finest works presently available. Unfortunately there are not many books written on this subject.

CHAPTER THREE

USING THE EPHEMERIS: PART I

For purposes of this presentation, we will be using a ten-year ephemeris known as ***The American Ephemeris for 1991-2000,*** by Neil F. Michelsen. Only the midnight editions are available. This ephemeris is published by Astro Communications Services (ACS) of San Diego, California, and retails for $9.95.

For those who want a longer-term ephemeris, you can purchase ***The American Ephemeris For the Twentieth Century,*** also by Neil F. Michelsen of ACS in San Diego. This covers the period 1901-2000. The cost is $19.95. Midnight and noon editions are available, but for illustration purposes we will be using midnight editions of ephemerides during this text.

And finally, for those who are planning the way-out future (which is getting closer every day), ACS also has available a ***50-year Ephemeris for the 21st Century***, covering the years 2000-2050. It too is recommended and will become very useful as the next century arrives. The cost is $16.95. All are available through this publisher, MMA/Seek-It Publications in West Bloomfield, Michigan.

We will initially be referring to ***The American Ephemeris for 1991-2000***, but the figures used should be identical to those found in the 100-year, 20th century ephemeris, by same author.

LONGITUDE

DAY	SID. TIME	☉	☽	☽ 12 Hour	MEAN ☊	TRUE ☊	☿	♀	♂	♃	♄	♅	♆	♇
	h m s	° ' "	° ' "	° ' "	° '	° '	° '	° '	° '	° '	° '	° '	° '	° '
1 M	6 39 45	9♑ 50 21	16♉ 41 2	22♉ 43 58	22♎ 26.2	23♎R27.8	29♑ 8.4	12♒ 37.2	24♑ 10.2	29♐ 28.7	19♓ 23.7	29♑ 21.0	24♑ 40.7	1♐ 56.9
2 Tu	6 43 42	10 51 30	28 44 55	4♊ 44 16	22 23.1	23 22.9	0♒ 16.2	13 51.0	24 57.0	29 42.3	19 27.8	29 24.4	24 42.9	1 58.9
3 W	6 47 38	11 52 39	10♊ 42 24	16 39 40	22 19.9	23 15.0	1 19.0	15 4.8	25 43.8	29 55.8	19 32.0	29 27.8	24 45.2	2 0.9
4 Th	6 51 35	12 53 47	22 36 18	28 32 35	22 16.7	23 4.1	2 16.1	16 18.5	26 30.7	0♑ 9.4	19 36.2	29 31.2	24 47.4	2 2.8
5 F	6 55 31	13 54 56	4♋ 28 43	10♋ 24 52	22 13.5	22 50.8	3 6.6	17 32.1	27 17.5	0 22.9	19 40.6	29 34.7	24 49.6	2 4.7
6 Sa	6 59 28	14 56 4	16 21 12	22 17 51	22 10.4	22 36.0	3 49.7	18 45.8	28 4.5	0 36.4	19 45.0	29 38.1	24 51.9	2 6.6
7 Su	7 3 25	15 57 13	28 14 59	4♌ 12 45	22 7.2	22 20.9	4 24.5	19 59.3	28 51.4	0 49.9	19 49.5	29 41.5	24 54.1	2 8.5
8 M	7 7 21	16 58 21	10♌ 11 19	16 10 52	22 4.0	22 6.8	4 50.0	21 12.9	29 38.4	1 3.4	19 54.1	29 45.0	24 56.4	2 10.3
9 Tu	7 11 18	17 59 29	22 11 38	28 13 53	22 0.8	21 54.7	5R 5.5	22 26.4	0♒ 25.4	1 16.8	19 58.8	29 48.5	24 58.7	2 12.2
10 W	7 15 14	19 0 37	4♍ 17 54	10♍ 24 2	21 57.7	21 45.5	5 10.1	23 39.8	1 12.4	1 30.2	20 3.5	29 52.0	25 0.9	2 14.0
11 Th	7 19 11	20 1 45	16 32 40	22 44 15	21 54.5	21 39.5	5 3.3	24 53.2	1 59.5	1 43.6	20 8.3	29 55.5	25 3.2	2 15.8
12 F	7 23 7	21 2 53	28 59 15	5♎ 18 9	21 51.3	21 36.3	4 44.7	26 6.5	2 46.5	1 57.0	20 13.2	29 58.9	25 5.5	2 17.5
13 Sa	7 27 4	22 4 1	11♎ 41 29	18 9 46	21 48.1	21 35.3	4 14.3	27 19.8	3 33.6	2 10.3	20 18.2	0♒ 2.5	25 7.7	2 19.2
14 Su	7 31 0	23 5 9	24 43 32	1♏ 23 15	21 44.9	21 35.3	3 32.5	28 33.0	4 20.8	2 23.6	20 23.3	0 6.0	25 10.0	2 20.9
15 M	7 34 57	24 6 17	8♏ 9 21	15 2 9	21 41.8	21 34.9	2 40.1	29 46.2	5 7.9	2 36.8	20 28.4	0 9.5	25 12.3	2 22.6
16 Tu	7 38 54	25 7 25	22 1 52	29 8 34	21 38.6	21 32.9	1 38.5	0♓ 59.4	5 55.1	2 50.0	20 33.6	0 13.0	25 14.6	2 24.3
17 W	7 42 50	26 8 33	6♐ 22 8	13♐ 42 12	21 35.4	21 28.5	0 29.4	2 12.4	6 42.3	3 3.2	20 38.8	0 16.5	25 16.8	2 25.9
18 Th	7 46 47	27 9 40	21 8 12	28 39 21	21 32.2	21 21.1	29♑ 14.9	3 25.4	7 29.5	3 16.4	20 44.2	0 20.1	25 19.1	2 27.5
19 F	7 50 43	28 10 47	6♑ 14 35	13♑ 52 40	21 29.1	21 11.4	27 57.3	4 38.4	8 16.8	3 29.5	20 49.6	0 23.6	25 21.4	2 29.1
20 Sa	7 54 40	29 11 54	21 32 14	29 11 49	21 25.9	21 0.0	26 39.1	5 51.3	9 4.0	3 42.6	20 55.1	0 27.1	25 23.7	2 30.6
21 Su	7 58 36	0♒ 13 0	6♒ 49 54	14♒ 25 3	21 22.7	20 48.4	25 22.8	7 4.2	9 51.3	3 55.6	21 0.6	0 30.7	25 26.0	2 32.1
22 M	8 2 33	1 14 6	21 55 58	29 21 32	21 19.5	20 37.8	24 10.3	8 16.9	10 38.6	4 8.6	21 6.2	0 34.2	25 28.2	2 33.6
23 Tu	8 6 30	2 15 10	6♓ 40 48	13♓ 53 7	21 16.4	20 29.3	23 3.5	9 29.6	11 26.0	4 21.5	21 11.9	0 37.7	25 30.5	2 35.1
24 W	8 10 26	3 16 14	20 58 2	27 55 23	21 13.2	20 23.5	22 3.8	10 42.3	12 13.3	4 34.4	21 17.7	0 41.3	25 32.8	2 36.5
25 Th	8 14 23	4 17 16	4♈ 45 9	11♈ 27 31	21 10.0	20 20.4	21 12.3	11 54.8	13 0.6	4 47.2	21 23.5	0 44.8	25 35.0	2 37.9
26 F	8 18 19	5 18 18	18 2 50	24 31 34	21 6.8	20D 19.4	20 29.5	13 7.3	13 48.0	5 0.0	21 29.3	0 48.3	25 37.3	2 39.3
27 Sa	8 22 16	6 19 18	0♉ 54 15	7♉ 11 27	21 3.6	20R 19.5	19 55.7	14 19.7	14 35.4	5 12.8	21 35.3	0 51.9	25 39.5	2 40.6
28 Su	8 26 12	7 20 18	13 23 51	19 32 3	21 0.5	20 19.5	19 31.0	15 32.0	15 22.7	5 25.4	21 41.2	0 55.4	25 41.8	2 41.9
29 M	8 30 9	8 21 16	25 36 43	1♊ 38 29	20 57.3	20 18.2	19 15.0	16 44.2	16 10.1	5 38.1	21 47.3	0 58.9	25 44.0	2 43.2
30 Tu	8 34 5	9 22 13	7♊ 37 55	13 35 36	20 54.1	20 14.7	19D 7.5	17 56.4	16 57.5	5 50.6	21 53.4	1 2.4	25 46.3	2 44.4
31 W	8 38 2	10♒ 23 9	19♊ 32 4	25♊ 27 46	20♎ 50.9	20♎ 8.4	19♑ 8.1	19♓ 8.4	17♒ 44.9	6♑ 3.2	21♓ 59.5	1♒ 5.9	25♑ 48.5	2♐ 45.6

1st of Month Julian Day # 2450083.5 Delta T 59.2" Obliquity 23°26'14" SVP 05♓18'49" Galactic Center 26♐47.6 Chiron 13♎34.7

DECLINATION and LATITUDE

DAY	☉ DECL	☽ DECL	☽ LAT	☽ 12Hr DECL	☿ DECL	☿ LAT	♀ DECL	♀ LAT	♂ DECL	♂ LAT	♃ DECL	♃ LAT	♄ DECL	♄ LAT
1 M	23S 4	14N55	1S59	16N 4	21S42	1S24	18S46	1S49	22S20	1S 4	23S11	0N15	6S 9	2S 7
2 Tu	22 60	17 2	2 55	17 49	21 18	1 14	18 24	1 49	22 12	1 4	23 12	0 15	6 7	2 7
3 W	22 54	18 23	3 42	18 46	20 54	1 4	18 2	1 48	22 3	1 5	23 12	0 15	6 5	2 7
4 Th	22 49	18 55	4 19	18 53	20 30	0 52	17 40	1 48	21 54	1 5	23 12	0 14	6 3	2 6
5 F	22 43	18 37	4 44	18 10	20 6	0 39	17 17	1 47	21 45	1 5	23 12	0 14	6 1	2 6
6 Sa	22 36	17 31	4 58	16 40	19 42	0 25	16 53	1 47	21 36	1 5	23 12	0 14	5 59	2 6
7 Su	22 29	15 39	4 58	14 27	19 19	0 10	16 29	1 46	21 27	1 5	23 12	0 14	5 58	2 6
8 M	22 22	13 7	4 45	11 38	18 57	0N 6	16 5	1 45	21 17	1 5	23 12	0 14	5 56	2 6
9 Tu	22 14	10 1	4 19	8 18	18 37	0 23	15 40	1 44	21 7	1 5	23 12	0 14	5 54	2 6
10 W	22 5	6 29	3 42	4 36	18 19	0 41	15 15	1 43	20 57	1 5	23 12	0 14	5 52	2 6
11 Th	21 57	2 39	2 54	0 39	18 2	0 59	14 50	1 42	20 46	1 5	23 12	0 14	5 50	2 5
12 F	21 47	1S23	1 56	3S24	17 49	1 18	14 24	1 41	20 36	1 5	23 12	0 14	5 48	2 5
13 Sa	21 38	5 25	0 52	7 24	17 37	1 37	13 57	1 40	20 25	1 5	23 11	0 14	5 45	2 5
14 Su	21 28	9 19	0N17	11 9	17 29	1 56	13 31	1 38	20 14	1 5	23 11	0 14	5 43	2 5
15 M	21 17	12 52	1 26	14 25	17 23	2 14	13 4	1 37	20 2	1 5	23 11	0 14	5 41	2 5
16 Tu	21 6	15 48	2 33	16 58	17 21	2 31	12 36	1 35	19 51	1 5	23 11	0 14	5 39	2 5
17 W	20 55	17 52	3 33	18 30	17 20	2 46	12 9	1 34	19 39	1 5	23 11	0 13	5 37	2 5
18 Th	20 43	18 49	4 20	18 48	17 23	2 60	11 41	1 32	19 27	1 6	23 10	0 13	5 35	2 4
19 F	20 31	18 27	4 50	17 46	17 27	3 11	11 12	1 30	19 15	1 6	23 10	0 13	5 32	2 4
20 Sa	20 19	16 46	5 0	15 28	17 33	3 20	10 44	1 28	19 2	1 6	23 10	0 13	5 30	2 4
21 Su	20 6	13 54	4 49	12 7	17 41	3 26	10 15	1 26	18 50	1 6	23 10	0 13	5 28	2 4
22 M	19 53	10 8	4 17	8 1	17 50	3 30	9 46	1 24	18 37	1 6	23 9	0 13	5 25	2 4
23 Tu	19 39	5 49	3 29	3 34	18 0	3 31	9 17	1 22	18 24	1 5	23 9	0 13	5 23	2 4
24 W	19 25	1 18	2 29	0N57	18 11	3 30	8 47	1 20	18 11	1 5	23 9	0 13	5 21	2 4
25 Th	19 11	3N 8	1 22	5 15	18 21	3 27	8 17	1 18	17 57	1 5	23 8	0 13	5 18	2 4
26 F	18 56	7 16	0 12	9 10	18 33	3 22	7 47	1 15	17 44	1 5	23 8	0 13	5 16	2 3
27 Sa	18 41	10 55	0S56	12 31	18 44	3 16	7 17	1 13	17 30	1 5	23 7	0 13	5 13	2 3
28 Su	18 26	13 58	1 59	15 14	18 55	3 8	6 47	1 10	17 16	1 5	23 7	0 13	5 11	2 3
29 M	18 10	16 19	2 56	17 13	19 6	2 60	6 16	1 8	17 2	1 5	23 7	0 13	5 9	2 3
30 Tu	17 54	17 55	3 43	18 24	19 16	2 50	5 46	1 5	16 47	1 5	23 6	0 12	5 6	2 3
31 W	17S38	18N42	4S20	18N47	19S26	2N40	5S15	1S 2	16S33	1S 5	23S 6	0N12	5S 4	2S 3

DAY	♅ DECL	♅ LAT	♆ DECL	♆ LAT	♇ DECL	♇ LAT
1	20S48	0S32	20S42	0N29	7S56	12N52
5	20 46	0 32	20 41	0 29	7 56	12 53
9	20 43	0 32	20 39	0 29	7 57	12 54
13	20 40	0 32	20 38	0 29	7 57	12 55
17	20 37	0 32	20 36	0 29	7 57	12 56
21	20 34	0 32	20 34	0 29	7 57	12 57
25	20 31	0 32	20 33	0 29	7 57	12 58
29	20S28	0S32	20S31	0N29	7S57	12N59

☽ PHENOMENA

PERIGEE/APOGEE

dy	hr	kilometr
5	12 a	406526
19	23 p	357252

MAX/0 DECL

dy	hr mn	
4	3:18	18N56
11	15:51	0
18	5:27	18S51
24	6:56	0
31	10:51	18N47

MAX/0 LAT

dy	hr mn	
6	12:22	4S59
13	18:16	0
19	23:24	5N00
26	4:13	0

VOID OF COURSE ☽

LAST ASPECT			☽ INGRESS		
2	1am19	♅△	2	♊	2am30
3	5pm54	♄□	4	♋	2pm57
7	2am55	♅☍	7	♌	3am31
9	0am33	♀☍	9	♍	3pm30
12	1am54	♅△	12	♎	1am56
14	7am36	♀△	14	♏	9am31
16	5am39	☽⚹	16	♐	1pm26
17	11pm21	♄□	18	♑	2pm 8
20	12pm52	☽☌	20	♒	1pm16
21	5am 2	♂☌	22	♓	1pm 3
24	7am54	♆⚹	24	♈	3pm38
26	2pm 5	♆□	26	♉	10pm17
29	0am15	♆△	29	♊	8am43
31	5am 1	♄□	31	♋	9pm12

dy	hr mn		PHASE
5	20:52	14♋48	○
13	20:46	22♎57	☾
20	12:52	29♑45	●
27	11:15	6♉48	☽

DAILY ASPECTARIAN

Day	Aspect	Time
1 M	☿☌♅	4am34
	☽⚹♄	5 24
	☿⚺♃	8 44
	☽△♂	3pm53
	☽△♆	3 55
	♂☌♆	4 27
	☉⚼☽	5 42
	☿ ♒	6 7
2 T	☽△♅	1am19
	☽⚻♃	1 57
	☽△☿	3 21
	☽☍♇	6 29
	☽#♀	6pm 6
	♀∠♃	8 26
	☽⚼♆	10 4
3 W	☽⚼♂	0am 3
	☉⚻☽	2 35
	☿∥♅	7 14
	♃ ♑	7 23
	☽⚼♅	7 36
	☽△♀	9 49
	☽⚼☿	12pm19
	☿∥♆	12 35
	☽□♄	5 54
	☿⚹♇	5 59
4 Th	☽⚻♆	4am26
	☽⚻♂	8 27
	☽⚻♅	2pm 3
	☽☍♃	3 33
	☽⚻♇	7 8
	☽⚼♀	7 37
	☽⚻☿	9 2
5	☉☍☽	8pm52
6 S	☽⚼♇	1am32
	☽⚻♀	5 26
	☽△♄	6 54
	☽#♀	11 36
	☽☍♆	5pm14
	♀⚺♄	8 35
7 Su	☽☍♂	1am19
	☽☍♅	2 55
	☽⚻♃	5 18
	☽△♇	7 51
	☽☍☿	12pm54
	☽⚼♄	1 19
8 M	♂☌♅	3am39
	☉∠♇	4 51
	☿∠♄	6 19
	♂ ♒	11 3
	☽⚼♃	11 58
	☉⚻☽	2pm50
	☽⚻♄	7 33
9 T	☽☍♀	0am33
	☽⚻♆	5 33
	☽#♇	2pm23
	☽⚻♅	3 12
	☽⚻♂	5 28
	☽△♃	6 23
	☽□♇	7 55
	☿SR	9 45
	☉⚼☽	11 23
10 W	☽⚻☿	1am43
	☽#♄	4 4
	☽⚼♆	11 17
	♂⚺♃	12pm42
	☿∠♄	4 35
	☽⚼♅	8 50
11 Th	☽⚼♂	0am56
	☉⚹♄	2 48
	♀⚺♆	3 23
	☽⚼☿	6 41
	☽☍♄	7 1
	☉△☽	7 22
	♂⚹♇	8 38
	♂∥♅	12pm55
	☽OS	3 51
	☽△♆	4 31
	☽⚻♀	5 53
	♂∥♆	6 50
12 F	☽△♅	1am54
	☽□♃	5 45
	☽⚹♇	6 19
	♅ ♒	7 13
	☽△♂	7 41
	☽△☿	10 34
13 S	☽⚼♀	1am19
	☽∥♄	2 0
	☽∠♇	10 28
	☿☌♂	11 21
	☽∥♇	3pm23
	☽⚻♄	4 2
	♃⚺♇	6 33
	☉□☽	8 46
14 Su	☽□♆	0am48
	☽△♀	7 36
	☽□♅	9 44
	☽⚺♇	1pm45
	☽⚹♃	2 1
	☽□☿	2 55
	☽□♂	6 20
	☽⚼♄	7 14
15 M	☿⚺♃	1am 7
	☽∥♀	1 18
	♀ ♓	4 31
	☿⚹♇	6 58
	♀⚺♅	8 1
	♂∠♄	11 41
	☽∠♃	4pm43
	☽△♄	9 29
16 T	☉☌♆	2am55
	☽⚹♆	5 27
	☉⚹☽	5 39
	☿⚺♀	6 43
	☽⚹♅	1pm51
	☽⚹☿	2 59
	☽□♀	4 29
	☽∥☿	4 31
	☽☌♇	5 28
	☽⚺♃	6 26
17 W	☽⚹♂	0am35
	☿☌♅	4 3
	♀□♇	4 31
	☽∠♆	6 26
	☉∠☽	8 25
	☿ ♑	9 38
	☽∠☿	1pm45
	☽∠♅	2 36
	♀⚹♃	8 22
	☽□♄	11 21
18 Th	☽∠♂	2am18
	☽⚺♆	6 42
	☉⚺☽	10 19
	☽⚺☿	11 55
	☽⚺♅	2pm43
	☉∥♅	4 9
	☉∥♆	4 17
	☽⚺♇	6 3
	☽☌♃	7 36
	♅∥♆	8 43
	☽⚹♀	9 15
	☉☌☿	9 41
19 F	☽⚺♂	3am23
	☽∥☿	3pm25
	☽∠♇	5 41
	☽∠♀	10 50
	☽⚹♄	11 1
20 S	☽☌♆	6am 3
	☽☌☿	7 23
	☉☌☽	12pm52
	☽☌♅	2 1
	☽⚹♇	5 14
	☉ ♒	6 54
	☽⚺♃	7 22
	☽∠♄	10 42
	☿☌♆	11 0
21 Su	☽⚺♀	0am24
	☽☌♂	5 2
	☉☌♅	7 22
	☽∠♃	7pm28
	☽⚺♄	10 40
22 M	☽∥♀	2am26
	☽⚺☿	3 20
	☽⚺♆	5 43
	☿∠♀	9 3
	☽∥♇	12pm24
	☽⚺♅	2 2
	☉⚺☽	4 11
	☽□♇	5 15
	☽⚹♃	8 7
23 T	☽∠☿	2am 8
	☽∥♄	2 22
	☽☌♀	5 5
	☽∠♆	6 22
	☉⚹♇	8 1
	☽⚺♂	8 21
	☽∠♅	3pm 0
	☉∠☽	7 3
	♀∠♆	8 46
24 W	☿∥♂	0am 7
	☽☌♄	0 34
	☽⚹☿	1 46
	☽ON	6 56
	☽⚹♆	7 54
	☽∠♂	11 26
	☽⚹♅	4pm54
	☿⚹♄	7 2
	☽△♇	8 15
	☉⚹☽	11 7
25 Th	☽□♃	0am 4
	☽#♄	12pm12
	☽⚺♀	2 7
	☉⚺♃	2 55
	☽⚹♂	3 45
	♀∥♇	4 22
	☽⚼♇	11 17
26 F	☽#♀	2am53
	☽#♇	4 15
	☽□☿	4 18
	☽⚺♄	6 24
	☽□♆	2pm 5
	☽∠♀	8 42
	☉∥☿	9 54
	☽□♅	11 55
27 S	☽⚻♇	3am22
	☉∠♄	6 58
	☽△♃	8 21
	☽∠♄	10 56
	☉□☽	11 15
	♀⚺♂	3pm 4
28 Su	☽□♂	4am 8
	☽⚹♀	4 37
	♀∠♅	8 9
	☽△☿	11 40
	☽⚼♃	2pm 0
	☽⚹♄	4 22
29 M	☽△♆	0am15
	☽#♂	8 8
	☽△♅	10 44
	☽☍♇	2pm11
	☽⚼☿	5 1
	☽⚻♃	8 21
	☉#☽	11 57
30 T	☉△☽	3am49
	☽⚼♆	6 20
	☿SD	10 12
	☽⚼♅	5pm 1
	☽△♂	8 8
	☽□♀	11 7
	☽⚻☿	11 11
	☿⚹♀	11 52
31 W	☽□♄	5am 1
	♀∥♄	9 49
	☽⚻♆	12pm44
	☉⚼☽	12 57
	☽⚻♅	11 32

Example 1: A page in the American Ephemeris, showing planetary positions for January, 1996

Every page in this ten-year ephemeris covers a one-month period, from January, 1991 through December, 2000. Each page provides a daily position of each planet, the Sun, the Moon, and the Moon's North Node (True and Mean) as seen from Earth, at midnight of that day, based on Greenwich Mean Time (GMT). The planet's position at midnight, GMT, is measured in terms of its tropical zodiacal position. Keep in mind that if you are calculating to Eastern Standard Time (i.e. New York City, the New York Stock Exchange, and/or Commodities Exchanges for precious metals like Gold, Silver and Copper, as well as Crude Oil, Sugar, Cocoa, Coffee and Cotton), these figures must be adjusted to reflect the 7:00 PM time of the night before. In other words, the figures given apply also to 7:00 PM, EST, the day before.

Let's look at a typical page in this ephemeris and see how it works. Let's look up January 1, 1996 (see example 1). Notice that the far left hand column gives the day of the month (1-31), and the day of the week on which that date falls. January 1, 1996 falls on a Monday, as indicated by the 'M' next to the '1' (January 1).

The next column gives Sidereal Time. Since we are interested in geocosmic signatures, and not in calculating horoscopes (as in astrology, per se), we will not be using this column. If you are interested in learning to calculate an actual horoscope, then this column is important. There are several fine books out on this subject, including ***The Only Way To Learn Astrology...Parts 1 and 2*** by Marion March and Joan McEvers. Both authors, though Astrologers, have great personal experience in the field of financial markets.

The next column lists the daily position of the Sun (☉), as seen from Earth, in a tropical zodiac. Note that there are three columns of numbers here. The first is for the degrees, the second for the minutes, and the third for the seconds, of spatial arc. On January 1, 1996, you will see the Sun (☉) is 9° Capricorn (♑) 50' 21". That means at midnight, GMT, on January 1, 1996, the Sun (as seen from Earth) is positioned at 9 degrees of Capricorn, 50' minutes, and 21" seconds. Bear in mind that there are only 30 degrees to a sign (like Capricorn), so that on January 1, the Sun is about 1/3 of the way through the zodiac sign of Capricorn.

The next two columns give the midnight and noon (GMT) positions of the Moon (☽). On January 1, 1996, the midnight position of the Moon is 16 degrees of

Taurus (♉), 41 minutes and 02 seconds of arc. At noon, GMT, the same day, the Moon has moved forward to 22 degrees Taurus, 43' and 58". You can see that in 12 hours, the Moon has moved forward just slightly over 6 degrees. It moves about 1 degree every two hours, or about 30'/hour (this is approximate; it varies slightly from this number during the month).

The next columns give the position of the Mean ☊ and True ☊, or the Moon's North Node (☊). Although this is not a planet, or celestial body in space, it is nevertheless important in understanding long-term cycle changes, as will be discussed later. Note that January 1, 1996, the Mean Node is located at 22° ♎ 26.2'.

The next column belongs to Mercury (☿). On January 1, 1996, GMT, midnight, Mercury is located at 29° Capricorn (♑) 8.4'. Following that you see the midnight GMT positions for Venus (♀), Mars (♂), Jupiter (♃), Saturn (♄), Uranus (♅), Neptune (♆), and Pluto (♇).

As you go down any of the planetary columns, you may note a date in which that planet changes signs. The sign change shows between the degrees and minutes of the planet for that date. For instance, on January 21, 1996, you will see the Sun changes signs, from Capricorn (♑) to Aquarius (♒). Likewise on January 16, under Venus, you will note that Venus changes to Pisces, as it shows 0°♓59.4'. Changes of signs will also be noted for Mercury on January 18, Mars on January 9, Jupiter on January 4, and Uranus on January 13. Can you identify what signs those are? If not, do not worry. We will cover that section shortly (Chapter 5).

CHAPTER FOUR

UNDERSTANDING PLANETS

Before continuing with our use of the ephemeris, let's change our direction a bit by spending some time on understanding the planets. In order to understand the effects of planetary mechanics upon financial markets, it is useful to first of all commit to memory the order and symbol of each planet, plus Sun and Moon, used in geocosmic studies. Not only will this help in understanding market psychology, but this particular study is also very fascinating for most people on a personal level. Keep in mind that many of these are the same symbols and order used by astrologers in their work for over 2000 years.

They are, in order, as shown on the next page.

Now go back to the ephemeris, and note the same planets on the top of the page, in the same order we have just memorized.

What do these planets mean in the study of financial astrology? To get an understanding, let's look at their cycle length, and show how those cycles have been found in other aspects of Man's environment and world (reality). Bear in mind that there are really two types of planetary cycle lengths we can discuss. The first is *heliocentric*, which refers to the length of the planets' orbit around the Sun, as seen from the Sun. The second is *geocentric*, which is the cycle of the planet as seen from the Earth. For the planets inside of the Earth's orbit (Mercury and Venus), the differ-

THE ORDER, SYMBOLS, AND NAMES OF THE PLANETS

☉ - SUN

☽ - MOON

☿ - MERCURY

♀ - VENUS

♂ - MARS

♃ - JUPITER

♄ - SATURN

♅ - URANUS

♆ - NEPTUNE

♇ - PLUTO

☊ - MOON'S NORTH NODE

Table 1: The Planets

ence between these cycles is quite significant. However for the other planets, which are outside of the Earth's orbit, the difference in cycle length is not significant.

The majority of cycles reported herein - and others - can be found in two books titled: ***Cycles-Selected Writings***, by Edward R. Dewey, and ***Catalogue of Cycles: Part 1- Economics***, by Louise L. Wilson. Both of these books are available through The Foundation For The Study Of Cycles, Inc., 900 West Valley Road, Suite 502, Wayne, PA 19087. Others have been reported by independent researchers like Walter Bressert, Jeanne Long, and myself, as noted. Even the cycles reported by Dewey and Wilson that were originally discovered by other researchers are mentioned herein.

THE SUN (☉)

Let's start with the Sun. As seen from the Earth, the Sun appears to move 360 degrees per year. Thus it is an "annual cycle" (one orbit cycle per year). In actuality, it is the Earth that makes one revolution around the Sun per year. The nature of the Sun in these studies is to "illuminate" the other planets it enters into an aspect with (more on aspects later), or even the "sign" it is in (more on signs later). The Sun's complete cycle is thus one year, and its cycle within each sign is approximately 30 days.

The following cycles in human activity have been identified which move in cycles close in length to the Sun's annual cycle:

11.1-13.9 months: Industrial Stock Prices (Dewey, 1952; Merriman, 1988)
11.52-month: Sales of certain companies (Dewey, 1951)
1 - year: Purchasing power of poultry (Pearson & Myers, 1944)

The following cycles in human activity have been identified which correspond closely to the time of a Sun's ingress through each sign (28-31 days):

28-day: Stock prices (Seager, 1962)
34 days: Raw sugar prices (Dewey & Dakin, 1947)

THE MOON (☽)

The Moon's cycle is 27-29 days. That is how long it takes to make one complete rotation around the Earth (27-1/3 days). However, it also has a "New Moon" cycle of 29.53039 days - the length of time it takes between New Moons (conjunction of the Moon to the Sun). The Moon's nature is to "change", according to planets it aspects, and signs it transits through (more on transits later). As it takes 27-1/3 days to go through the entire 360 degrees zodiac, it can be seen that its average length of time in any one sign (30 degrees, or 1/12 of zodiac) is about 60 hours, or 2-1/2 days.

The following cycles in human activity have been identified which coincide closely with the periodicity of the Moon:

28 days: Stock prices (Seager, 1962)
29.5 days: Birth of infants (Jackson, 1939-45)
29.6 days: Earthquake activity throughout the world (Davidson, 1940)

MERCURY (☿)

Mercury's cycle around the Sun (heliocentric) is 88 days, or 12.6 weeks. It spends approximately 5-11 days in one sign (heliocentrically) and approximately 19 days in one sign geocentrically, when it is not stationary due to retrogradation. In astrology, Mercury represents communication, but in business language, it pertains to commerce, the act of buying and selling. When Mercury is prominent by aspect to other planets, there tends to be an increase of buying and selling (volume), according to the planet being aspected or the sign Mercury is in. Mercury is also "mental", so it can describe the things of mental interest to the market community on any given day, or during the time period in which it transits a particular sign.

The following cycles in human activity which have a periodicity close to that of Mercury have been identified:

12.31 weeks: General Motors common stock prices (Shirk, 1962)
12.5 weeks: Odd lot short sales (Viele, 1962)
12.94 weeks: Industrial stock prices (Dewey, 1951)

The 5-11 day period it takes Mercury to transit from one sign to another in a heliocentric approach, has been reported to coincide with short-term trend changes in a variety of commodity markets (i.e. grains) by independent researcher Jeanne Long.

VENUS (♀)

Venus has a cycle of 225 days, or 32.2 weeks, in its orbit around the Sun. It spends, on average 18-19 days heliocentrically in a sign, and about 24-26 days geocentrically in a sign, when it is not stationary due to retrogradation. Venus is said to rule things of "value" in astrology (in addition to the traditional matters of love and romance). It pertains to money matters and agreements, and in general when Venus is prominent by aspect, greater value is placed upon those matters ruled by the other planets in aspect. Specifically Venus is said to govern Copper and Sugar prices. In stocks, it pertains to cosmetics and beauty aids.

The following cycles in human activity have been identified, which are very close in periodicity to that of Venus:

32 weeks: Westinghouse Electric common stock prices (Shirk, 1961)
32.25 weeks: Industrial stock prices (Dewey, 1952; Blackett and Wilson, 1936-38)

It takes Venus about three weeks to transit from one sign to another in heliocentric astrology. Walter Bressert has identified a three-week trading cycle (low to low) in precious metals. Jeanne Long suggests that prices of various financial markets may reverse on the Venus ingress, heliocentric.

MARS (♂)

Mars is the first planet outside of the Earth's orbit. Therefore all the following planets will have cycles of greater than one year in their orbit around the Sun. Mars takes 687 days, or 98 weeks, or 23 months to orbit the Sun. It spends approximately 43 days (6 weeks) in a geocentric sign, except when it is stationary. The nature of Mars is aggressive and competitive. It is, in mythology, the God of war. Mars is frequently prominent during those days in which there is an increase in international tensions, perhaps even threats of war. In markets, volume tends to increase when Mars is present, and with it comes sharp swings in price (volatility). Mars rules steel, defense stocks, and the meats (in commodities).

The following cycles in human nature have been identified, which closely approximate the cycle lengths of Mars:

23 months: Industrial stock prices (Dewey, 1952)
Textile production (Peterson, Myers, Brandow, 1939)
Cotton consumption (Bassie 58)
Wholesale Commodity prices (Frickey, 35)
Semi-durable goods production (Newbury, 1952)

It takes Mars about 43 days (6 weeks) to transit each sign of the zodiac in geocentric terms. A cycle of 6-weeks has been identified by both Bressert and Merriman in precious metals, and by Merriman in stock prices, Corn, Wheat, and Soybean prices.

JUPITER (♃)

Jupiter is the largest planet in our solar system. It orbits the Sun about once every 12 years (actually it is 11.9 years). It takes approximately 11-13 months to transit through one sign, so this "ingress" cycle is nearly the same as the Sun's annular cycle. Jupiter's nature is to inflate, to coincide with feelings of optimism and euphoria. Typically planets ruled by the sign Jupiter is in will go up in price, and during those days when it is in aspect to other planets, prices of certain stocks and commodities will tend to soar upwards. Jupiter is a co-ruler of oil (crude).

The following cycles in human activity have been identified that coincide closely with Jupiter's orbital period around the Sun:

11.67-year: Depressions (Langham, 1954)
12 year: Industrial stock prices (Dewey, 1951, 1954, and Szartrowski, 1948)
Wheat prices (Beveridge, 1927)
Cigarette stock prices (Wilson, 1962)
12.08-year: Bank deposits (Wardwell, 1927)

SATURN (♄)

Saturn is the last of the visible planets in our solar system. Its orbital cycle around the Sun is 29.5 years. It spends approximately 2-1/2 years in each sign as it makes this journey. Saturn's nature is to "contract" and "depress", just the opposite of Jupiter. When Saturn is prominent, those stocks and commodities ruled by the sign it is in either tend to decline in price, or supplies of it become diminished. When Saturn is prominent by aspect in any given day, certain commodities or stocks may reach a low in price. Oftentimes volume is low during these days as investors tend to be governed more by fear (Saturn) than greed (Jupiter).

The following cycles in human activity have been identified which closely approximate cycles related to Saturn's movement through the cosmos:

29.7 years: Famines (Nakame, Japan, 1957)
30 year: Industrial stock prices (Dewey, 51)
Residential building construction (Caincross, 1934)

Saturn spends approximately 2.4 years, or 27-30 months, in each sign as it transits through the zodiac. There are many 27-30 month cycles in human activity that have been reported, including:

27 month: Gold prices (Merriman, 1982)
Canadian Gold mining stocks (Dewey, 1954)
27.5 month: USA stock prices (Dewey, 1954)
27.6 month: Copper share prices (Shirk, 1961)
28.9 month: General business activity (Flood, 1940)
29.2 month: Copper prices (Dewey, 1953)
29.28 month: Industrial stock prices (Dewey, 1951)
30 month: Egg prices (Funk, 1931)

URANUS (♅)

Uranus is the first of the "newly discovered" planets, and like the other two, it is not visible to the naked eye from Earth. Uranus' cycle around the Sun is 84 years. It takes about 7 years to move through each sign of the zodiac. The nature of Uranus is to surprise, to disrupt, to bring forth the unexpected. Sudden sharp and unexpected moves in financial market prices frequently happen when Uranus is active by aspect. The moves may be sharp, but not necessarily long lasting. In fact, it can and does coincide with "whipsaw" behavior, volatility, where prices move sharply in both directions, changing direction suddenly and sharply, even within the same day. Support and resistance, defined by technical analysis, may easily break during these Uranian days.

The following cycles in human activity that may relate (in time) to the cycles of Uranus have been identified:

84 years: Wheat prices (Appel, 1950)
Wholesale commodity prices (Appel, 1950)
Social and political unrest (Dewey, 1951)

There are numerous cycles which correspond to Uranus's 7-year transit interval through each sign of the zodiac, including:

7 years: Business recessions (Mitchell, 1927; Merriman, 1994)
Butter prices (USDA Yearbook of Agriculture, 1930)
Combined stock prices (Shirk, 1958)
General business activity (Petty, 1962, Mitchell, 1927)
Trade activity (Jevons, 1909)

NEPTUNE (♆)

Neptune is the second of the "far out" planets. Its orbit around the Sun lasts 164.8 years, and it spends about 14 years in each sign. Neptune coincides with rumors and illusions, hopes and wishes that are not necessarily based upon facts. When Neptune is prominent, traders may be focusing upon the "wrong" matters, or upon rumors that turn out to be untrue. For many, it is difficult to make objective market decisions when Neptune is prominent by aspect. Not all the facts are present, and those that are may not be accurate. Neptune is the other ruler of oil (crude), and also relates to rain and moisture, which can affect crop prices..

The following cycles in human activity that closely approximates Neptune's 14-year periodicity through each sign have been identified:

14 years: Cattle production (Zimmerman, 1951)
Industrial stock prices (Woods, 1946)

It should also be noted that Neptune travels through the "Earth" signs every 54 years (more on this in the chapter on Signs). In his book "The Sign Of The Times" (Llewellyn, St. Paul, MN, 1984), Stan Barker points out the presence of economic downturns (depressions) during these periods. Perhaps this ties into the well-known "Kondratieff Cycle", or "K-Wave", a 54-year economic recession cycle reported by Russian economist Nikolai Kondratieff.

PLUTO (♇)

Pluto is the last known (at this time) planet in our solar system. It has an erratic orbit that takes 248.4 years to complete around the Sun. However it may spend between 14-26 years in any given sign. As it goes through Scorpio and Sagittarius (1982-2009), it takes about 14 years each. Pluto's nature is to coincide with threat of damage or destruction, through nature or man-induced (i.e. terrorism). It is explosive. When Pluto is prominent by aspect, various markets may reverse and begin rather long trend runs. It terminates old trends, and begins new ones. Sometimes it coincides with break outs of long standing support or resistance levels in price, if the market is close by at the time of a Pluto aspect.

There are very few cycles that have been identified in human activity that approximates Pluto's periodicity. The closest is:

242 years: Famines (Grassman, 1957)

THE MOON'S NORTH NODE (☊)

The Moon's Nodal cycle lasts 18.73 years. It spends approximately 18-19 months in each sign as it makes this journey through the zodiac. There is not much attention paid to the Moon's Nodes in astrology, so it's relevance has yet to be determined. Yet of all the planetary cycles discussed, there are more cycles in human activity that have been reported that closely approximate the Nodal cycle of the Moon than any other.

Some of these include the following:

18-18.7-years: Building activity per capita (King, 1938)
Building activity and construction (Daniels, 1935, Dauten, 1954)
Building permits per capita (Riggelman, 1935)

New building permits (Burns and Mitchell, 1946)
Real estate activity (Hoyt, 1933)
Bank credit (Warren and Pierson, 1937)
Industrial stock prices (Tripp, 1948, Merriman, 1987)
Major panics (Warren and Pierson, 1937)
Wheat acreage (King, 1938; Dewey and Dakin, 1947)
Furniture production (Dewey and Dakin, 1947)
General business activity (Hays, 1937)
Silver prices (Merriman, 1991)

A feature to keep in mind with cycles of all types (especially planetary cycles), is that sub-cycles exist in which the major cycle can be divided by the numbers 2, 3, or 4. In other words, Pluto's 248-year cycle has two subcycles of 124 years, three subcycles of 83 years (which approximates Uranus' full cycle), and four cycles of about 62 years. Perhaps the most well-known are the quarter cycles of Saturn, which last about 7 years each. Another well-known cycle is the 54-year "K-Wave", or "Kondratieff Cycle", which measures severe world recessions/depressions. This coincides to a third of the Neptune cycle, and seems to unfold when Neptune transits through Earth signs, as discussed under Neptune.

Furthermore there are cycles that exist between planets to one another. For example, each planet conjuncts every other planet in a rhythmic periodicity. Jupiter and Saturn conjunct, for instance, every 20 years. There are several well-documented 20-year cycles. In fact, there are several cycles in human activity that coincide with cycles of planetary combinations, but they are too numerous to mention here. Aspects between planets, however, will be covered shortly in another section. They (aspects between planets) are the crux of market timing, but to calculate these, we need first of all to understand the planets (this chapter) and the measurement qualities of the signs (next chapter).

At this time, it would be a good idea to quiz yourself on the symbols and order of the planets in the solar system. Perhaps take a blank piece of paper, and see if you can write the planets and symbols in their order. When done, check your results with that of Table 1, on page 13. It will be necessary to commit these planetary symbols to memory if you plan to use geocosmic signatures for market timing.

CHAPTER FIVE

THE SIGNS OF THE ZODIAC

As the planets travel around the Sun in their predictable orbits, they do so in the foreground of a circular band of constellations known as "the Zodiac." It is against the zodiac background that a planet's position is measured and identified. There are twelve (12) constellations which make up the zodiac, also known as "signs", and each is given a space of 30 degrees. In actuality, these "constellations" may contain more or less than 30 degrees in the heavens, and they do not form a perfect circular backdrop for the planets motions. But as "signs" used in the study of astrology, they are measured 30 degrees each, starting with the season of Spring (around March 21 of every year).

Now it should be mentioned that there is a difference between "signs" and actual constellations. When one looks at a planet in the heavens, the constellation in the background may not be the same as the "sign" it is said to be in, due to the continuous "wobble" or "tilting" phenomenon of the Earth on its axis over a 25,200 year period. As the Earth "tilts", or "wobbles", the view of the planets from Earth are altered slightly every year. In fact, every 72 years, the "tilt" `accounts for a 1 degree difference between the "sign" and the "constellational" position of a planet as seen from Earth. This is not significant to our study, for we are identifying a planet's position by "sign" only, which is more a measurement of the seasons upon Earth (thus relevant to human activity), and not by "constellation" (which might pertain more to a universal approach of analysis). This is only brought up because inevitably as you proceed with the study of astrology, you will hear of so-called "scientists" who may use this fact as a reason why astrology cannot work. Such an argument says nothing about astrology, but instead only shows the critic's ignorance of the mechanics used in astrology - a reference based upon seasons as the Earth rotates around the Sun, and not upon the "tilt" of the Earth on its axis and the view that affords of the constellations in the heavens.

The "signs" of the zodiac are very useful in the study of geocosmic signatures related to financial markets for many reasons. Most important perhaps is their value in measuring distances between planets, so that we can ascertain "aspects" that are in effect. As you will see shortly, "aspects" are the crux of identifying potential turning points in markets. It is the basis for "market timing", ala geocosmic studies.

Therefore it is again important for the learner to memorize both the order and the symbols of the signs of the zodiac. The order, and symbols, for these "signs of the zodiac" are shown on the following page (Table 2).

As you can see, there are 12 signs to the zodiac. The zodiac begins with Aries and ends with Pisces. Aries is the first sign, and Pisces is the 12th. You could start the circle again for mathematical reasons, by referring to Aries as not only the 1st sign, but also the 13th, or 25th, signs.

Each sign also has 30 degrees. All 12 signs added together account for the 360 degrees in the circle. Thus when you see a planet in the ephemeris listed as 15° Taurus (♉), this means it is half way through the second sign of Taurus, which like all signs, contains 30 degrees. It also means it is 45 degrees into the zodiac, since it covers the 30 degrees of Aries, plus the first 15 degrees of Taurus. In like fashion, a planet in 10 degrees of Sagittarius would be at the 1/3 point of the 30 degrees of Sagittarius. It has 20 more degrees to go before it moves into the next sign of Capricorn. Likewise, since Sagittarius begins the 9th sign of the zodiac, we could say it is in the 250th degree of the zodiac (8 signs, times 30 degrees each, plus 10 degrees of Sagittarius). This, then, is how we measure distances between planets.

SIGNS OF THE ZODIAC: THEIR ORDER AND SYMBOLS

♈ - ARIES

♉ - TAURUS

♊ - GEMINI

♋ - CANCER

♌ - LEO

♍ - VIRGO

♎ - LIBRA

♏ - SCORPIO

♐ - SAGITTARIUS

♑ - CAPRICORN

♒ - AQUARIUS

♓ - PISCES

Table 2: Signs of the zodiac

Also note that each degree contains 60' of arc. Thus in the ephemeris, it might say something like: 25° Capricorn (♑) 38'. If the planet moved forward 22' more, it will be in the next degree, or 26° Capricorn (♑) 00'. Again, this is important for measurement. For purposes at this time, it will be sufficient just to round off to the nearest degree. Thus if we have a planet that shows more than 30' of arc, we will round off to the next degree. If it shows less than 30' of arc, we will simply use the whole degree that is showing. If we were actually calculating a horoscope for someone, we would be more concerned with minutes and perhaps seconds of arc. But in the study of geocosmic signatures related to market analysis, we are not concerned (at least not now) with horoscopes. Thus we are not concerned with the greater body of study known as astrology, which takes into account horoscopes. We are simply interested in "aspects" - when they occur, and what they mean to various markets in terms of potential reversals. The aspects between planets is what we primarily mean when we use the term "Geocosmic studies." And to determine those times of aspects, we need to know the signs of the zodiac, which enables us to calculate the distance between any two planets.

At this time, it would be a good idea to quiz yourself, to make sure you can list the order and the symbols for the 12 signs of the zodiac as they appear in Table 2. Again, it will eventually be necessary to commit these signs and their order to memory if you plan to use geocosmic signatures in your efforts to time potential reversals in financial markets. Before proceeding with the next chapter, please consider pausing right now and embark upon this exercise. It may also be wise to list the planets, their symbols, and order as they appear in Table 1 before continuing on to the next chapter.

MAJOR ASPECTS AND THEIR SYMBOLS

☌ - CONJUNCTION (0°)

□ - SQUARE (90°)

△ - TRINE (120°)

☍ - OPPOSITION (180°)

MINOR ASPECTS AND THEIR SYMBOLS
(NOT IMPORTANT FOR THIS STUDY)

⚺ - SEMI-SEXTILE (30°)

∠- SEMI-SQUARE (45°)

⚹ - SEXTILE (60°)

⚼ - SESQUIQUADRATE (135°)

⚻ - QUINCUNX (150°)

Table 3: Aspects and their distances.

CHAPTER SIX

USING THE EMPHEMERIS PART II: DETERMINING ASPECTS

Aspects are specific spatial distances of arc that might exist between any two planets (or points in space). The times in which aspects between two planets are in effect is potentially a period of time in which a reversal in the trend of a market may unfold.

The major aspects we will study are shown on the previous page in Table 3. They are (not in order of distance, but in an order that may be easier to learn):

Conjunction: 0 degrees.
Opposition: 180 degrees
Square: 90 degrees
Trine: 120 degrees
Sextile: 60 degrees* (somewhere between a major and minor aspect)

There are of course other aspects (especially the sextile, but also the semi-sextile, semi-square, sesquiquadrate. quincunx, quintile, etc.). But the major aspects that seem to correlate with the most noteworthy changes in market prices are the four basic aspects listed on the top of Table 3: the conjunction, opposition, square and trine, and in many cases, the sextile. Thus for purposes of this book, those will be the primary ones studied. These alone will be sufficient to get you started on becoming a more accurate market timer, using geocosmic studies.

Now before we discuss aspects in detail, let's learn how to find the distance between any two planets. This is very important, and even though you may have a computer to do this work for you, it is still essential to understand the mechanics of how this is done. Otherwise it may not really mean anything of great importance to you. So take the time to learn these mathematical calculations if you wish to increase your skills as an astute market analyst and market timer.

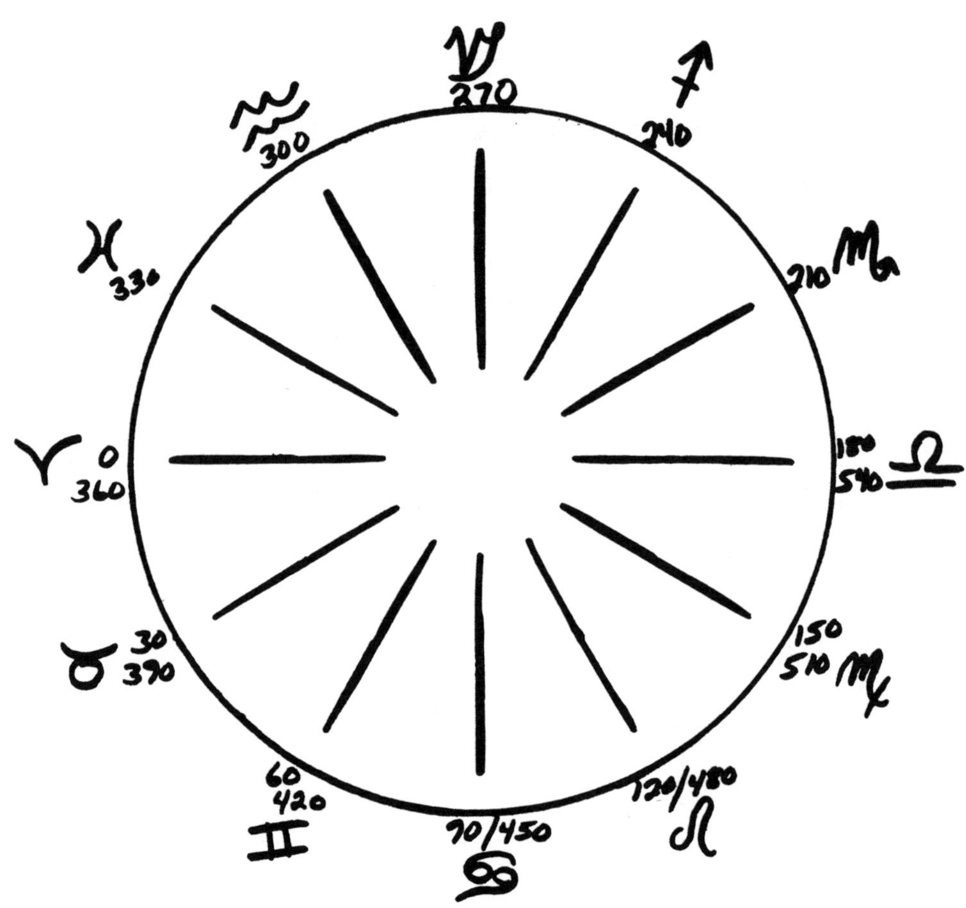

Figure 1: An Aries chart, for purposes of calculating aspects between planets

First of all, understand that the planets move in a counter-clockwise direction as seen from Earth. Look at the circle in Figure 1, and note that the signs of the zodiac (on the outside of the circle) proceed in a counter-clockwise direction. Notice also that this circle is divided into twelve (12) equal segments, for there are 12 signs to the zodiac. Also note that each segment contains 30° each, and that these are cumulatively added as we go from one sign to the next. This is done so that the subtraction and addition procedures are easier to see.

We begin our task of finding aspects by determining the shortest distance between any two planets in question. Let's call the planet furthest ahead in this shortest arc, in a counter-clockwise direction, the "leading planet", and the other planet, the "trailing planet."

The formula to find the distance between any two planets, then, is:

Leading Planet (sign and nearest degree)
- Trailing Planet (sign and nearest degree)

To show how this is done, let's go to an example. Let's look up January 1, 1996. Remember, the degrees and minutes of every planet in the ephemeris for that day is based upon midnight, GMT. If we were calculating for a New York market, these degrees and minutes would pertain to 7:00 PM, EST, or 8:00 PM, when daylight savings time is in effect, for the previous day (December, 31, 1995). If you wish to be exact, you will have to calculate a planet's hourly movement, and add the necessary minutes of arc to the GMT midnight position to correlate with the period of time in which that market is opened during that day. This is done by finding the daily movement of each planet, and dividing by 24 (hours in a day). This gives you the hourly movement in minutes of arc. You then multiply that figure by the number of hours later that the New York markets are open (if using 9:00 AM, EST, you would multiply the hourly movement by 14 hours, since 9:00 AM, EST, is 14 hours after 7:00 PM, EST of the previous day. 9:00 AM, EST is also 14 hours after midnight, GMT, when time zones are taken into account).

Do not get alarmed at this point. You do not have to do this calculation. Because of other techniques to be covered later on (chapter on "Using the

Aspectarian"), it is not necessary to pursue that type of accuracy at this time. For now, we simply want to learn how to estimate the distance between planets (closest degree is good enough), and from there, ascertain whether or not a major aspect is in effect.

Now, using an Aries chart (as in Figure 1), put each planet (by nearest degree) in your chart. Make sure it is sorted correctly by sign position. In other words, round off each planet as it appears on January 1 to the nearest degree, except the Moon. Since

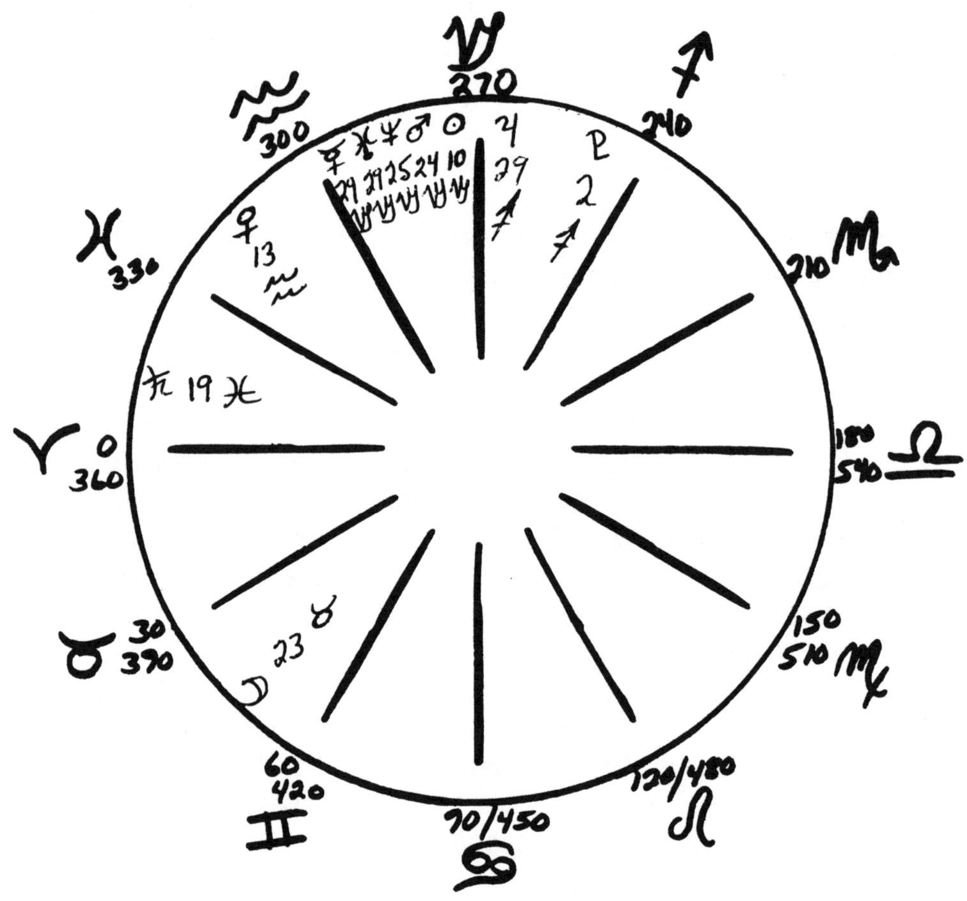

Figure 2: Example of planets for January 1, 1996 (GMT) in Aries chart

the Moon moves about one degree every two hours, you may want to approximate where it would fall 14 hours later in New York, or about 9:00 AM (i.e. add 7 degrees to the Moon and put it in). You can look to Figure 2 to see how these planets should be placed into the Aries chart for calculations purposes.

Note that you have, in counter-clockwise order, Pluto (♇) 2° (♐), Jupiter (♃) 29° Sagittarius (♐), Sun (☉) 10° Capricorn (♑), Mars (♂) 24° Capricorn (♑), Neptune (♆) 25° Capricorn (♑), Uranus (♅) 29° Capricorn (♑), Mercury (☿) 29° Capricorn (♑), Venus (♀) 13° Aquarius (♒), and Saturn (♄) 19° Pisces (♓). The Moon, after calculations of adding 7 degrees to the midnight position (or one degree to the noon position, which equates to 7:00 AM, EST), comes out to 23° ♉ (Taurus). From this point onwards, all signs and planets will be given according to their symbols, so you must have Tables 1, 2 and 3 memorized by now.

Let's say we want to find the distance between Jupiter and Saturn. The shortest arc, counterclockwise, is Jupiter to Saturn, where Saturn is the "leading planet" and Jupiter the "trailing planet." Let's put it down in our format for a calculation:

Saturn	**19♓**	**or,**	**349°**
- Jupiter	**29♐**	**or,**	**269°**

We know Pisces is the 12th sign. The full 11 signs which precede it cover 330 degrees 30° per sign, times 11 signs). If we add the additional 19 degrees of Saturn's position in Pisces, we come to a total of 349° for Saturn's position. We can do the same with Jupiter at 29°♐. Sagittarius is the 9th sign of the zodiac. Thus the first 8 signs cover 240 degrees. The additional 29 degrees gives a total zodiacal position of 269°. Thus the calculation now reads:

Saturn	**349°**
- Jupiter	**269°**
Total =	**80°**

Now when we subtract, we get a total of 80 degrees as the distance between Jupiter and Saturn on January 1, 1996.

This is the long-hand method to find the distance between any two planets on any given day. Whenever they are 0, 180, 90, or 120 degrees apart (or even 60 degrees), there is an exact aspect on that day. However, an "orb" may be allowed. It doesn't have to be exactly those degrees to be "in influence." Some analysts will use an 8-10 degree orb; others like MMA, prefer a 3 degree orb. Or, when it is exact, MMA may state that "within three trading days, a reversal is likely to occur." The orb may be in time (number of days away), or spatial arc (degrees from exact aspect).

Now let's look at another way to determine whether or not an aspect is in effect. You can take the degree of every planet, and see if any two planets are within three degrees (regardless of sign) to one another. If they are, chances are they may be in one of these four (or five) major aspects.

For example, if two planets are within three degrees of one another, and in the same sign, they are in conjunction (☌) to one another. If two planets are within three degrees, but in opposite signs (six signs apart), they are in opposition (☍) to one another. If they are within three degrees, and three signs apart, they are in square (□). If they are within three degrees of each other, and four signs apart, they are in trine (△) aspect to one another.

Looking at our example on January 1, 1996, note that ♂ and ♆ are within three degrees of one another and in the same sign (♑). Mars and Neptune are thus in conjunction to each other. Likewise ☿ and ♅ are in ☌ aspect.

Now look at the ☽ to ♂ or ♆. All are within three degrees. But the ☽ in ♉, is four signs away from Mars and Neptune in Capricorn. Four signs apart, but within three degrees, is a trine aspect between the Moon and Mars, as well as Moon and Neptune. This is an easier way to calculate aspects. But the important thing to determine is this: when is an aspect in effect? When is it exact? Then we know that within three trading days (and oftentimes exactly on the date), there is likely to be a reversal in some market(s). This is the crux of market timing using the principles of Geocosmic studies.

CHAPTER SEVEN

USING THE ASPECTARIAN

There is an easier way to determine the exact date two planets make a major aspect to one another. In fact, there are two ways that are easier. But before describing those two ways, please keep in mind the reasons why we went through this exercise of calculating distances between two planets. First, it is important to understand how the mechanics work. It familiarizes you with the techniques - as well as signs and planets - that are used in Financial Astrology. Secondly, this technique will help you develop an "eye" for approximating when an aspect is coming into effect, simply by looking at any ephemeris. If you know what signs the planets are in, and what their approximate degrees are, then you know almost instantly whether a major aspect is close at hand.

Rather than using fractions and thereby calculating "the long way" as to when an aspect is in exact formation, some of the current day ephemerides provide an "aspectarian" for each day. An "aspectarian" shows, in chronological order, the precise time during each day when an exact aspect has formed.

In ***The American Ephemeris For The 20th Century (1900-2000)***, there is no aspectarian provided. If you are using this ephemeris, you have to estimate the time (or date) of a major aspect. However, ***The American Ephemeris 1991-2000*** (or any ten-year ***American*** ephemeris) does provide an aspectarian at the bottom of each page (month). It is titled as the **DAILY ASPECTARIAN**, and appears in the lower quarter of the page. Once again, look at the page for January, 1996 (shown in Example 1 on page 10), and you will see this section.

Now let's look at this Aspectarian. Note the first column starts with January 1, a Monday. The first aspect shown that day is ☿☌♅ at 4:34 AM. Remember this is GMT time, so in New York, it would occur 5 hours earlier (11:34 PM, December 31, 1995). So the conjunction between Mercury and Uranus actually occurred at precisely 11.34 PM, December 31, 1995 in New York City, which is the same as 4:34 AM on January 1, 1996 in London.

Notice further along on that same date, Mars and Neptune conjunct at 4:27 PM, GMT (or 11:27 AM, in New York). Also notice later on that same day Mercury moves from Capricorn to Aquarius at 6:07 PM, GMT. This is shown as ☿ ♒. This is significant. This is known as a "sign change", or an **ingress of a planet**. Ingresses of planets are almost as important as aspects. They too can denote a trend reversal, for they indicate a change of thinking, or feeling, about the areas which the planets pertain too. In astrology, the planets denote the *activity,* but the signs describe the *arena* in which the activity takes place. Mercury, for instance, is the business activity. Capricorn tends to be an arena of government, politics. Business activity may be influenced by concerns for governmental regulations, decisions and policies during that period. As it moves into Aquarius, government concerns may "back off" the business community. Aquarius has more to do with freedom, and the relaxation of regulations. Such a change in the market psychology can have an impact upon various financial markets for the few weeks that Mercury transits through Aquarius.

When you see an aspect starting to form (simply by looking at the planetary positions in an ephemeris), you can then go to the aspectarian to determine *exactly* when it will unfold. You then have an exact point to start the measurement of a time band for a potential reversal that may pertain to markets related to those planets.

Now it is important to keep in mind that not all aspects are equal in their correspondence to potential reversals in financial markets. The general rule is that the influence (strength) of an aspect is proportionate to the length in time of its cycle. In other words, the longer it takes any two planets involved in an aspect to come into orb, the more potent its correspondence is likely to be upon major reversals in various financial markets. If Mars and Jupiter come together (conjunction) approximately every 26 months, then its corresponding influence to a market reversal will likely be greater than that of the Sun and Moon, which come together (conjunction) every 29-1/2 days.

The Moon, of course, is the fastest moving body that we observe in the calculations of daily aspects. Thus in any aspectarian, you will note that the majority of aspects on any given day will usually involve the Moon. These are referred to as "lunar aspects", and except for intraday trading, they are not given much attention. Their time of influence is generally no more than 2 hours either side of their aspect. Furthermore their correspondence to market reversals are usually minimal, except to day traders. A lunar aspect without an accompanying planetary aspect is not likely to result in what we call a "market reversal", as shown on daily bar charts.

"Planetary aspects" are much more significant. These refer to the aspects formed between the Sun and/or the planets, but not involving the Moon.

As you look over the aspects - via the aspectarian - in effect for January 1, 1996, you will note the following lunar aspects in effect (anything that has the Moon to it):

☽✶♄ 5:24 AM
☽△♂ 3:53 PM
☽△♆ 3:55 PM
☉□☽ 5:42 PM

If the markets were open that day, then there might some intraday activity within two hours either side of these lunar aspects. But by themselves, they are not considered powerful enough to warrant expectations of a major cycle reversal in any market. However, the planetary aspects, and the planetary ingresses of that day, do warrant consideration as possible correspondences to major market reversals, give or take three trading days. This is particularly true of markets that have a relationship to Mars/Neptune (crude oil and its products), Mercury/Uranus, and Mercury changing signs (grains). Changes of trends are not limited to just those markets that relate to the planets, for keep in mind that *any planetary aspect or ingress can coincide with a change in collective psychology.* Market participants are part of a group which has a *collective mindset*. Mindsets tend to change as aspects or ingresses are taking place, or at least within a few days.

The exception to this is when a long-term planetary cycle is forming (a cycle whose length of time is greater than, say, 30 months). A long-term planetary aspect does not usually coincide with a change in the collective psychology right at the moment it is happening. Major changes of collective psychology change over a period of time, not overnight. In astrology, the rule is 3-9° either side of the exact aspect is the time band during which the "change" or "events" unfold. Some astrologers prefer the longer orb (i.e. 8-9 degrees); others prefer the shorter orbs (even 1-3 degrees). It is the author's experience that 8-9 degrees seems effective when dealing with collective psychology, but 1-3 degrees seems sufficient to time any important "event" that may transpire related to that aspect. Thus at MMA, we prefer a 3° orb for outlining a time band for a potential market reversal. This too is modified in the case where several planetary aspects form within a short span of time (i.e. less than 12 days), which is known as a "cluster". In the event of a "cluster", we take the midpoint in time of all the aspects, and allow an orb of three trading days either side as a time band for a potential reversal.

For now, let's see an example of a short-term potential market reversal signature, and a long-term one. If you look in the aspectarian for January, 1996, you will see a "cluster" of short-term planetary signatures (aspects and ingresses) between January 15-21, 1996. They are:

Jan 15	♀ ♓	4:31 AM
Jan 16	☉☌♆	2:55 AM
Jan 17	☿☌♅	4:03 AM
	♀□♇	4:31 AM
	☿ ♑	9:38 AM
Jan 18	☉☌☿	9:41 PM
Jan 20	☉ ♒	6:54 PM
	☿☌♆	11:00 PM
Jan 21	☉☌♅	6:54 PM

The point midway within the "cluster" is January 18, 1996. Each of these geocsomic signatures are "short-term" Thus we would anticipate a reversal in trend in various financial markets within three trading days of January 18, or January 15-23, 1996. However, since none of these signatures between January 15-21 are "long-term", it is not likely that this period represents a major change in long-term collective psychology. The trend reversals might be of the 1-3 week variety, which is sufficient for a trader, but perhaps not for an investor.

Let's look at another example of using the aspectarian. Go into your ephemeris and look up August 20, 1993. Note that Uranus conjuncts Neptune at 7:45 AM, GMT, that day. This is a very long-term cycle. Its periodicity is 171 years. That's right, this conjunction only occurs every 171 years. It is the greatest planetary cycle that we will experience in our lifetime. You will note that it also happened two other times in 1993, due to the retrograde factor of these planets: February 2 (8:12 AM) and October 24 (8:19 PM). In fact, these two planets stay within a 9° orb for several years (1987-1999). It is over this long period of time that the psychology of the collective makes a major change. Very long-term cycles in many financial markets are likely to reverse during that period, but it is so long in effect that it may not be useful at all for trading purposes.

Let's illustrate this principle of market reversals correlating with geocosmic clusters in action. Let's look up the geocosmic signatures that were present near the high that formed on August 31, 1994, in the S&P futures market. An examination of the aspectarian will show the following planetary aspects:

Aug 28	♀□♆
	♃△♄
Aug 29	☿△♆
Aug 30	♀□♅
	♂△♄
Sep 1	♂△♃
	☉☍♄

The midpoint of this powerful cluster is August 30, 1994, just one day from that primary cycle crest that formed. The high that formed that day in the S&P futures was

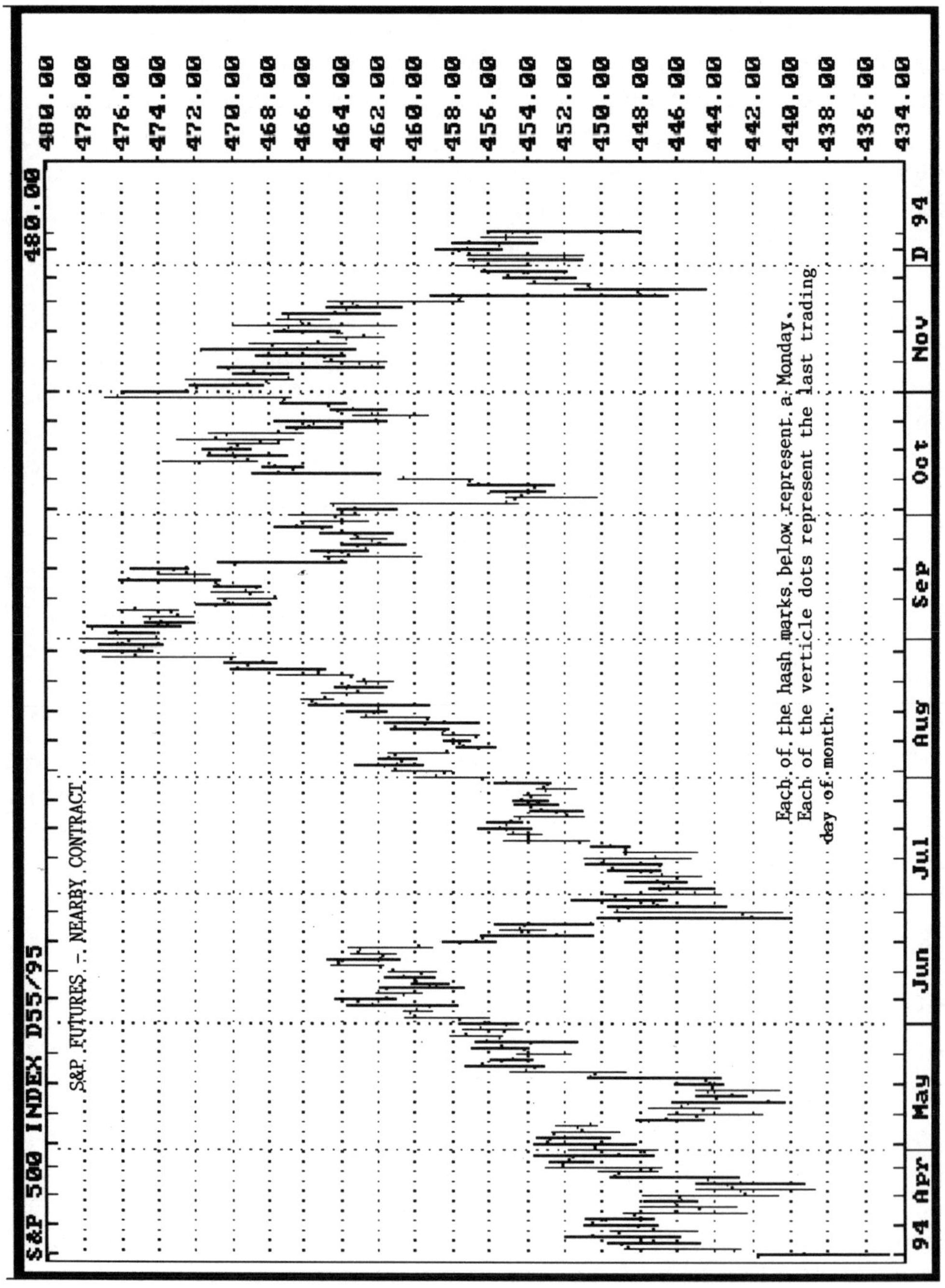
S&P 500 INDEX D55/95
480.00
S&P FUTURES - NEARBY CONTRACT
Each of the hash marks below represent a Monday.
Each of the verticle dots represent the last trading
day of month.
94 Apr
May
Jun
Jul
Aug
Sep
Oct
Nov
D 94
480.00
478.00
476.00
474.00
472.00
470.00
468.00
466.00
464.00
462.00
460.00
458.00
456.00
454.00
452.00
450.00
448.00
446.00
444.00
442.00
440.00
438.00
436.00
434.00

not seen again for several months (February, 1995). In fact, from that high, prices continued down rather sharply into late November, early December (there were clusters in effect then too).

At this point, it would be beneficial for the reader to look over any given month's aspectarian, and see if other "clusters" can be spotted. Another exercise that may prove valuable is to look up a daily chart of any stock index or commodity futures. Locate a significant crest (high price) or trough (low price). Mark down the dates, then go into the ephemeris and examine the aspectarian for a few trading days either side of those highs or lows. It is likely you will see a "planetary cluster" nearby.

CHAPTER EIGHT

USING COMPUTERS TO DETERMINE "CLUSTERS"

There is an easier way yet to identify potential reversal dates in financial markets by way of geocosmic signatures. It is by means of computer programs.

Calculating aspects by hand is obviously very cumbersome and time-consuming. Looking up aspects via the aspectarian in some ephemerides is easier and less time consuming, but still not as efficient as traders and market analysts might like. It still takes time to wade through all the aspects each day of each month in any given year, and determine which are important and which are not.

The ideal solution is to have a computer program that can pull up instantly, in chronological order, the various geocosmic signatures that can correspond to market reversals. There is such a program now available, known as ***F.A.R. - The Financial Astrological Research Program for Market Timing.***

This chapter may seem like an advertisement for FAR, but the fact is, FAR is the only software program available at this time which utilizes all the principles set forth in this book. If you find the market timing methods of this book to be of value, and you wish to access this information in the fastest and most efficient way possible, and you can afford it, then the FAR program is something to seriously consider.

Before showing how the FAR program works, let's set forth another principle of geocosmic studies. It goes like this: not all planets and their aspects have identical correspondence to all financial markets. Yet many planetary combinations do have similar correspondences with many financial markets.

To illustrate, consider the fact that aspects between the Sun and Jupiter have a pronounced and consistent correlation to market reversals in the U.S. stock markets. However the same planetary aspects between Sun and Jupiter do not have as great a correspondence to major market reversals in Gold and Silver.

In ***The Gold Book: Geocosmic Correlations To Gold Price Cycles***, I did a comprehensive study on the correlation of geocosmic signatures to various cycle highs and lows in the Gold market. This study set out to determine the "consistency" and the "power" of each geocosmic signature in the Gold market. "Power" was defined according to the type of cycle present during the orb of an aspect (primary, one-half primary, major, or trading cycles, in which primary was given greatest weight). This study showed that there were only a few geocosmic signatures that consistently correlated with a cycle of at least a "half-primary" or greater average rating (a scale of 1-10 was developed, and those whose signatures were greater than 9.00 were considered "one-half primary or greater" in power). Several others had a consistent correlation, but their "power" was less (7.50 or greater).

Those that were the most powerful and consistent were labeled **Level One**. Those that were consistent in some sort of reversal, but not as powerful, were labeled **Level Two** (or Three). What proved to be most interesting since that study was completed in 1982, is that when clusters of **Level One** signatures are present, almost all financial markets are vulnerable to reversals of trends - not just Gold. When the psychology of the group changes, it has a domino effect that eventually touches many other markets, as most financial markets do not usually operate in isolation from one another. We know that to be true through our personal experiences as traders and investors, but this concept may be somewhat foreign to astrologers. Astrologers tend to believe that certain planets and certain signs have rulership - and hence correspondence - over particular markets. Thus when a major aspect occurs involving Venus, astrologers will tend to look only at the Sugar or Copper markets. However, even though Sugar and Copper may be greatly effected under Venus transits, so too are other markets at the same time. It's not just Sugar and Copper. Any aspect may coincide with a collective psychological shift, and when that occurs, any market making a new three-week high or low may be vulnerable to a reversal. It is as if the energy that led to the trend has climaxed at the time of the aspect, and that energy now goes into remission as a new energy starts up.

But back to **Level One** and **Level Two** signatures. For the most part, these signatures consisted of 1) specific and certain planets in aspect to one another or 2) specific planets in "station". We have already discussed aspects. A "station" has to do with those times when a planet appears to be changing its direction (orbit) around the Sun, as seen from Earth. These "stations" are known as "retrograde" or "direct" dates. To illustrate this concept, imagine you are driving a car in the left lane of a circular track, going 50 miles per hour. In the right lane ahead of you is a car traveling at the rate of 40 mph. As you look ahead, you know that car is going forward (i.e. "direct motion"). Eventually you pull even with that car, and slowly begin to pass it. From that moment onwards, it will appear as if that car is going backward (i.e. "retrograde") in relationship to you. When you reach somewhere on the opposite side of that track from the other automobile, it will again appear as if that other vehicle is in front of you (instead of behind you). Its motion is again "direct", or forward, in relationship to you. Those two moments - when the other vehicle appeared to start a backward (retrograde) motion, and then again when it appeared to start a forward (direct) motion, are known as "stations."

Planets do the same thing in relationship to Earth as they orbit around the Sun. There are moments in those orbits when the planet will "appear" to be starting a backward, or retrograde, motion. In the ephemeris, this is noted with the symbol 'R' in the planet's column, on the date that this phenomenon begins. To illustrate, turn back to page 10, example 1, showing a page from the ephemeris of January, 1996. Look down the Mercury column to January 9. You will see the letter 'R' between the degrees and minutes of Mercury. On January 9, 1996, Mercury goes "retrograde". If you look at the aspectarian below, you will see this takes place at 9:45 PM, GMT. The date a planet goes retrograde is known as a "station", and in the case of many planets, can coincide with a trend reversal.

Now look at the Mercury column on January 30, 1996. Between the degrees and minutes of Mercury on that date you will see a 'D'. This stands for "direct". The retrograde motion is over, and Mercury resumes its "direct" motion on this day. The aspectarian shows that this change in motion occurred at 10:12 AM on January 30, 1996. This too is known as a "station", and likewise may correlate to a market reversal. Thus "stations", like "aspects" and "ingresses", fall into the category of a geocosmic signature. And, just as certain planets in aspect are assigned a Level One or Two value, so too are certain planets when they make a "station." A Venus station (going retrograde or direct), for instance, is a very powerful Level One signature in almost all financial markets, whereas a Mercury station may not be so powerful and consistent in its correlation with significant market reversals in most financial markets.

When Level One signatures are in effect - and particularly when a "cluster" containing them is in effect - the possibility of a market reversal is great. Obviously in this beginners book we will not go into the details of all Level One and Level Two signatures. If you are interested, then it is advisable to read both ***The Gold Book***, as well as ***Secrets of a Silver Trader: The Sun, Moon and Silver Market***, both available through MMA/Seek-It Publications.

The FAR program does many things, but one of the most useful and easy to use features is that known as the *MMA Studies*. In this option there are several choices, including: **Level One, Level Two**, and **Ingresses**. When you pull up any one of these directories, you have the option to choose any particular signature (like, say, Venus/Uranus), or a combination of all the signatures included in that directory (i.e. **All Level Ones**, or **All Level Twos**, or **All Ingresses**). Once you choose, you can then pick a starting date and an ending date, and the FAR program will give you a listing (or printout) of your choice in chronological order.

To illustrate, let's assume we wanted to see if there were any clusters of Level One signatures present between January 1, 1995-August 8, 1995. It is our belief that clusters of Level One signatures would likely correspond to a major reversal of many financial markets, within a period of three trading days of their midpoint, and we want to know when to anticipate such a reversal.

To do this via the FAR program, you simply choose *MMA Studies* from the main directory. On the next screen, you choose the directory titled *Level One*. Under here, you get a listing of all the individual Level One signatures, or *All*. Since we wish to locate clusters, we will choose *All*. The program will now provide a chronological

All Level One Aspects

Date	Time	Planet	Event		Planet	Position
Jan 2, 1995	(15h48m 8s)	Venus	is Sextile	to	Uranus	25 Sc 35
Jan 2, 1995	(16h27m42s)	Mars	goes Retrograde	at	....	2 Vi 40
Jan 9, 1995	(16h27m42s)	Venus	is Square	to	Mars	2 Sg 21
Jan 16, 1995	(19h20m54s)	Sun	is Conjunct	to	Uranus	26 Cp 25
Jan 25, 1995	(20h13m25s)	Mercury	goes Retrograde	at	....	21 Aq 16
Feb 1, 1995	(18h51m56s)	Venus	is Trine	to	Mars	26 Sg 49
Feb 16, 1995	(0h 6m 6s)	Mercury	goes Direct	at	....	5 Aq 37
Mar 1, 1995	(17h16m37s)	Venus	is Conjunct	to	Uranus	28 Cp 50
Mar 3, 1995	(16h10m44s)	Mercury	is in Opposition	to	Mars	15 Aq 56
Mar 3, 1995	(21h37m 0s)	Pluto	goes Retrograde	at	....	0 Sg 36
Mar 9, 1995	(13h27m 1s)	Jupiter	is Trine	to	Mars	14 Sg 35
Mar 14, 1995	(10h 0m48s)	Venus	is in Opposition	to	Mars	13 Aq 48
Mar 20, 1995	(12h 6m18s)	Sun	is Sextile	to	Uranus	29 Pi 37
Mar 24, 1995	(12h19m25s)	Mars	goes Direct	at	....	13 Le 10
Apr 1, 1995	(7h 1m 0s)	Jupiter	goes Retrograde	at	....	15 Sg 23
Apr 9, 1995	(17h22m59s)	Mercury	is Trine	to	Mars	14 Ar 40
Apr 12, 1995	(12h 1m30s)	Mars	is Trine	to	Jupiter	15 Le 11
Apr 20, 1995	(17h52m18s)	Sun	is Square	to	Uranus	0 Ta 23
Apr 22, 1995	(7h 9m52s)	Venus	is Sextile	to	Uranus	0 Ar 24
Apr 26, 1995	(3h26m53s)	Mercury	is Square	to	Mars	18 Ta 41
Apr 27, 1995	(17h26m 0s)	Neptune	goes Retrograde	at	....	25 Cp 33
May 5, 1995	(2h44m 0s)	Uranus	goes Retrograde	at	....	0 Aq 28
May 12, 1995	(1h45m 7s)	Venus	is Trine	to	Mars	24 Ar 19
May 17, 1995	(2h34m12s)	Venus	is Square	to	Uranus	0 Ta 25
May 21, 1995	(16h35m 8s)	Sun	is Trine	to	Uranus	0 Ge 22
May 24, 1995	(4h 1m57s)	Mercury	goes Retrograde	at	....	18 Ge 22
Jun 10, 1995	(10h28m 2s)	Venus	is Trine	to	Uranus	29 Ta 57
Jun 13, 1995	(4h23m32s)	Mars	is Square	to	Jupiter	9 Vi 1
Jun 15, 1995	(0h49m41s)	Mars	is Square	to	Mercury	9 Vi 58
Jun 17, 1995	(1h57m59s)	Mercury	goes Direct	at	....	9 Ge 49
Jun 21, 1995	(8h57m40s)	Venus	is Square	to	Mars	13 Ge 17
Jun 27, 1995	(6h56m13s)	Saturn	is Sextile	to	Neptune	24 Pi 41
Jul 3, 1995	(7h43m13s)	Mercury	is Square	to	Mars	19 Ge 46
Jul 6, 1995	(2h47m 0s)	Saturn	goes Retrograde	at	....	24 Pi 45
Jul 11, 1995	(9h21m 2s)	Mars	is Trine	to	Neptune	24 Vi 19
Jul 21, 1995	(12h39m 0s)	Sun	is in Opposition	to	Uranus	28 Cn 30
Jul 27, 1995	(11h54m16s)	Mercury	is Sextile	to	Mars	3 Le 45
Jul 28, 1995	(2h 3m32s)	Venus	is in Opposition	to	Uranus	28 Cn 14
Jul 30, 1995	(11h14m36s)	Mars	is Sextile	to	Jupiter	5 Li 33
Aug 2, 1995	(11h46m 0s)	Jupiter	goes Direct	at	....	5 Sg 32
Aug 6, 1995	(12h11m48s)	Venus	is Sextile	to	Mars	9 Le 50
Aug 8, 1995	(8h39m 0s)	Pluto	goes Direct	at	....	27 Sc 49

Example 2: All Level One signatures in effect from January 1, 1995-August 8, 1995, via the FAR program

printout, a listing of all the Level One signatures in effect between January 1, 1995 - August 8, 1995. A sample of this printout appears on the previous page, example 2. Notice the cluster of Level One signatures present between March 1-24, April 21-27, May 12-24, June 10-27, July 3-11, and July 21-August 8. In each of these clusters, there are no more than 6 trading days between at least two Level One signatures. These time bands can then be narrowed down by doing the same thing with the *Level Two,* and *Ingress* choices. When we finish making our time bands for potential reversals based upon the clusters of geocosmic signatures, we then pick the date midway within this cluster, and allow an orb of three trading days. This then becomes our "critical reversal" date, and its orb.

Using a computer program like FAR saves a lot of time. It makes for more efficient analysis. As stated before, it is not necessary to have a computer program to calculate critical reversal dates via the study of geocosmic signatures. You can do it simply with the use of an ephemeris that contains an aspectarian, or by hand.

The purpose of this book is to demonstrate how the basic principles of geocosmic studies can enhance one's market timing skills. It is to show how aspects are determined, and then how they are used to forecast potential times for market reversals. As such, it is an introductory book on the subject. It is not intended as an advanced manual. If you find this subject to be of interest, and more importantly to be of value in your trading or investing, then you may want to consider either more advanced studies, or the FAR program. For further information, please feel free to contact the publisher, MMA/Seek-It, at the number or address listed in the front of this book.

In the meantime, may you experience much success in your trading!

APPENDIX

THE SIGNS OF THE ZODIAC IN ASTROLOGY

In the study of astrology, their are four basic principles involved in analysis: the planets, the signs of the zodiac, the houses of the horoscope, and the aspects between planets. The planets are the most important factor in understanding the study of astrology. Besides the fact that it is the planets that comprise the makeup of an any aspect, it is also the relationship of the planets to the signs of the zodiac, and houses of the horoscope, that provide the groundwork for much of the delineation.

Just as the planets orbit around the Sun (and Earth, from a geocentric perspective) against the background of the constellation signs, so too do the planets represent the foreground of life experiences, against the background of our environment and attitudes, symbolized by the signs and houses. In other words, in the study of astrology, planets represent the activities of life - the behavior of the person and the events he/she tends to encounter - while the signs represent the background - or arena - in which those activities unfold. In a sense, the signs modify the activities signified by the planets. They also describe the environment, or arena of life, in which the events of life unfold.

This is also true in the field of financial astrology. The planets can indicate the activity of the financial community, such as buying, selling, low volume, high volume, volatility, or congestion. But the signs of the zodiac, in which those planets appear, tend to describe which categories (arenas of life) of markets that are likely to be effected. Perhaps in the field of equities (the stock market) is this concept most useful. Jupiter, for instance, represents inflation, growth, and increase. Whatever sign it is transiting through can point to an area of the financial community - or stock sector - which may either increase in price (stock) or supply (commodity). The opposite would be true of the sign Saturn transits through. Sectors represented by that sign may be vulnerable to a price decline, and commodities ruled by that sign might find a tightening of their supplies.

The following is intended to provide the reader with a sense of the psychological dynamics ascribed to the signs of the zodiac, as well as their correspondence to various sectors of the stock market.

Aries (♈): The key psychological principles of Aries include independence, assertiveness (aggression), and the drive to initiate. Its nature is energetic, impulsive, and competitive. It tends to foster an environment of quick and perhaps instinctive action. In world affairs (Mundane Astrology), or an a personal level, it may engage it tough rhetoric, anger, hostility, and disputes when negative.

When planets are transiting through Aries, markets tend to pick up in trading activity. Volume typically increases. Aries may have a correspondence to defense, sports, and steel companies in terms of the stock market.

* Note: the word "transiting" means "position of planets on that day." For instance if you were looking at the position of the planets today, you could refer to them as "today's transits." If you were to refer to a time when "planets are transiting Aries", you would mean a day in which planets are in the sign of Aries.

Taurus (♉): The key psychological principles of Taurus include security, possessiveness, retention, and appreciation. Its nature tends towards caution and conservatism. It will tend to hold onto something rather than sell it. It is more likely to relate to investments than to trading. It also tends towards resistance to change.

When planets transit through Taurus, markets tend to be in congestion. The financial community is not apt to act rashly, but rather conservatively. If prices were to break below support or above resistance, a sense of panic could emerge because of the "security" issue of Taurus. Otherwise volume tends to be stable and market prices orderly. Stocks ruled by Taurus include banks, financial institutions and investment management, holding companies, packaging, and containers.

Gemini (♊): The key psychological concepts of Gemini include intellectualization, displacement, projection, and love of variety. Its nature is to seek knowledge, and then to relate (communicate) that information. It will also attempt to rationalize or explain things in a manner that makes it appear objective or "out of the loop" (it doesn't like being blamed). It represents a love of learning, and oftentimes finds it difficult to focus on one thought or project at a time (easily distracted).

When planets transit through Gemini, financial markets tend to be volatile and given to short, sharp price swings ("whip-saws"). Stocks ruled by Gemini include the automotive, diversified operations, communications, telecommunications, telephones, newspapers, magazines, media and books, and transports categories.

Cancer (♋): The key psychological principles of Cancer include nurturing, caring, dependency, and loyalty. It tends to be family-oriented, seeking close intimate relationships that can be provided in a family setting. It is also protective of others. When attacked in any way, it can become very defensive and easily hurt. Its nature is very emotional and sensitive, and it seeks comfort.

When planets transit through Cancer, markets players may tend to react emotional and out of loyalty. Thus they are not prone to sell, much like when planets transit through Taurus. Interestingly enough, though, if markets break through support or resistance areas in either Taurus or Cancer, participants tend to get frightened (fear), and large price movements (especially declines) can and do happen here. Stocks sectors related to Cancer include agricultural operations, residential building, foods, motels, hotels, restaurants, supermarkets, household appliances, furniture, real estate development, home furnishings, utility water supplies, and dairy.

Leo (♌): The key psychological principles include creativity, leadership, immaturity, and recognition-hunger. Its nature is to seek attention. However it is also enthusiastic, affectionate and fun-loving, like a child.

When planets transit through Leo, a great deal of attention tends to be spotlighted on a specific target (stock sector). It brings flamboyant personalities to the fore - usually in a favorable light. Stock sectors that may coincide with the sign of

Leo include children's toys, gaming companies, games and hobbies, recreation, gambling, entertainment industry, and gold mining.

Virgo (♍): The key psychological concepts and attitudes related to Virgo include focus on detail, perfectionism, critical, helpful, and compulsive. The nature of the Virgo influence is to spotlight the small details. It can be very critical, in a constructive or "picky" way. It is cautious and logical, skillful and talented, like to help others but oftentimes is pessimistic and fearful about the future. It is also concerned about appearances and hygiene.

When planets transit through Virgo, many financial markets tend to suffer price declines (fear). Oftentimes they will find a bottom during these periods, especially in stocks (oftentimes a high in precious metals). Stock sectors related to Virgo include health care services, health maintenance organizations, office supplies, soap and cleaning products, maintenance and service, engineering, graphics, design, cereals, flours and grains, employment agencies.

Libra (♎): The key psychological concepts and attitudes related to Libra include sharing, relating, agreement, mediation, and acceptance-hunger. Its nature is to seek balance and moderation, peace and harmony. In this regard, it tends to see the opposite side of an issue that may be presented with a bias to only one side. It is compliant and agreeable, preferring to maintain a state of equilibrium as opposed to forcing an issue that may result in divisiveness. Libra also strives for beauty, both in its surroundings and its person.

When planets transit through Libra, financial markets tend to trade in a "trading range", or a somewhat wide congestion area. If stocks are moving up as planets go into Libra, they will usually correct during (and sometimes following) the transit into Libra. Stock sectors related to Libra include accounting, cosmetics, fashion, jewelry, apparel, sugar and refining, and law.

Scorpio (♏): The key psychological concepts and attitudes include reform, intensity. obsession, and power-hunger. The nature of Scorpio is to change things, hopefully to improve, but oftentimes the result is to destroy or terminate. There is a sense of "threat" or "crisis" present with Scorpio. Scorpio digs and probes, researches and investigates, until it finds the cause or source. To those it is probing oftentimes comes a terse threat to "get out", or rejection. If it is successful in its ventures, a sense of mastery comes about from the insight gleaned during the research.

When planets transit through Scorpio, there is oftentimes a "Wall of Worry" for financial markets to climb over. Frequently there is a world crisis in force that affects various financial markets. This is usually negative for equities and bonds (also a fear of default present). There could also be a threat to various food supplies in the world - fear of ruination caused by nature, but sometime man-made (terrorism). Stock sectors related to Scorpio include any financial lending institution, like banks, savings and loans, etc. Also relates to brokerage houses, oil and gas drilling, waste management, pollution control services, fertilizers, funeral services, coal mining, medical and surgical supplies, and insurance companies.

Sagittarius (♐): The key psychological concepts and attitudes include hope, exaggeration, freedom, space, and indulgence. The nature of Sagittarius is to expand and see things in a bigger light. It is very risk-oriented, tending greatly towards optimism and betterment of the present. It has a large degree of happiness potential which lends itself to charity and generosity. It represents quantity as opposed to quality. At its worst, it over-estimates and causes large losses.

When planets transit through Sagittarius, markets are given to large price fluctuations. "Blow-offs" are frequent here, where the value of something becomes grossly exaggerated. Much profit (or loss) can be encountered when planets transit Sagittarius, depending upon one's ability to capture the large move and get out in time, for surely the reversal will be large too. Stock sectors related to Sagittarius include travel (airlines), export-import, publishing, sports, religious and educational materials, and school supplies. It also deals with holding companies who are heavily invested throughout the world.

Capricorn (♑): The key psychological concepts and attitudes related to Capricorn include productivity, sense of accomplishment, control, and suppression. The nature of Capricorn is to worry, to be concerned with possible loss. It is also very disciplined and given towards making rules that allow it to be organized and structured. It is moral and duty-bound, with a heightened sense of morality, or "right and wrong." It can also be depressive and controlling. In Mundane Astrology, it rules government regulations and cold weather.

When planets transit through Capricorn, financial markets are prone to price declines as worries and anxieties increase. Oftentimes if a market has been trending up, it may enter into congestion as price activity and volume slows. If prices start down, though, they can accelerate quickly. Stock sectors ruled by Capricorn include paper and wood products, heavy equipment, farm machinery, cement, concrete, mining, building construction, rubber and tires, railroads, and manufacturing.

Aquarius (♒): The key psychological concepts and attitudes include progressive, inventive, individualistic, dissociative, and unpredictable. The nature of Aquarius is to encourage unique and perhaps non-conforming ways to view things. It is not traditional, but rather progressive, modern, and sometimes even bizarre. Hence the quality of "surprises" are associated with this sign.

When planets transit through Aquarius, unexpected movements in price are often seen (i.e. volatility). Stocks sectors related to Aquarius include computers, technology, electronics, electric products, laser systems and components, aerospace, and the media and cable, radio and television, and airlines.

Pisces (♓): The key psychological concepts and attitudes include passive, imaginative, helpful, and delusions or confusion. The nature of Pisces is to see things through altruistic or even idealistic eyes, perhaps with a sense for beauty and aesthetics. It tends not to see things as they are, but rather according to the way one wishes them to become. In Mundane Astrology, it rules hospitals, chemicals, medicines, alcohol, bodies of water, and rain.

When planets transit through Pisces, rumors often have a short-term effect on market prices. Markets can be volatile. When the "delusions" are moved aside, prices may return back to their dominant trend. Stock sectors related to Pisces include alcoholic and party beverages, chemicals, drugs, pharmaceuticals, hospitals, nursing care facilities, oil and gas, shipping, shoes, photography and cameras, movies and the film industry.

REFERENCES

1. Dewey, Edward R., CYCLES-Selected Writings, Foundation For The Study Of Cycles, 900 W. Valley Rd, STE 502, Wayne, PA 19087, 1970.

2. Wilson, Louise L., Catalogue of Cycles-Part 1: Economics, Foundation For The Study Of Cycles, Wayne, PA, 1964.

3. Bressert, Walter, and Jones, James, The Hal Blue Book, C/O Walter Bressert, P.O. Box 8068, Vero Beach, FL 32963, 1981.

4. Long, Jeanne, Basic AstroTech, PAS, 757 SE 17th St, #272, Ft. Lauderdale, FL 33316, 1988.

5. Merriman, Raymond A., The Gold Book: Geocosmic Correlations To Gold Price Cycles, MMA/Seek-It Publications, P.O. Box 250012, W. Bloomfield, MI 48325, 1982.

The S.O.S. Special Stock Market Report

By popular demand, MMA now has a new and exclusive stock market "Special Update" report. Issued every six week (8 times per year), this report provides an in-depth update of the phasing of longer-term cycles in the U.S. Stock Market. It also covers specific stocks that are prone to rise or fall in the intermediate-term, based upon an integration of cycles, geocosmics, and technical studies. Although short-term and options traders will find this valuable, SOS is designed with emphasis upon long-term investments in the U.S. Stock Market.

"Ray's work has class, integrity, and outstanding results. His accurate timing and analysis have an excellent cyclic technical foundation. The results of his cyclic analysis put him at the top of the ladder."

–David Marantette
Editor of the *Gold Stock Letter* and *Dear Dow Letter*

Subscription Prices: 1 year/sub: $150.00 •3 issue trial: $60.00 • Fax: add 50% if U.S. or Canada, 75% elsewhere. Postal delivery overseas add 10%. No extra cost for e-mail.

OTHER SERVICES

MMA WEEKLY and Daily Market Comments and Trade Recommendations (by Fax or E-mail only):

2-3 page update on 10 markets: Gold, Silver, U.S.A.. Stock Market, T-Bonds, D-Mark, Swiss Franc, Japanese Yen, Corn, Wheat, and Soybeans. Commentary on what to expect in each market in the forthcoming week or day, with specific buy and sell recommendations, by Raymond A. Merriman

Weekly Updates: $1,000.00/yr - $360.00/3 mo.
Daily Updates: $2,500/yr - $250.00/mo.
Fax: add 50% if U.S. or Canada, 75% elsewhere. No extra cost for e-mail.

Weekly Update of Japanese Nikkei - Fax or E-mail Only

Delivered by fax or e-mail every Friday afternoon (Eastern Time), this update gives in-depth analysis of what to expect in the Japanese Stock Market the following week. Highly accurate.

$1500.00/year - $450.00/3mo.
Fax: add 50% if U.S. or Canada, 75% elsewhere. No extra cost for e-mail.